Praise for
The 2 Minute Miracle of Blessing

It's over a decade since I was introduced to *The 2 Minute Miracle* by Dr. Lynn Reddick. I immediately recognized vital truth in his writings, and invited Lynn & Linda to come to New Zealand to teach in our Summer Schools in the three largest cities of our nation. Since then they have been back three more times, where they taught and ministered in 30 towns and cities across New Zealand. Their teaching and ministry have profoundly affected thousands of people across the denominational spectrum and beyond our shores.

Biblical blessing is a command from God Himself, and Lynn and Linda have demonstrated this with much fruit. People are still asking for copies of Lynn's book, so I am thrilled with this new edition that incorporates anecdotes of people's experiences. There are hidden blessings to be discovered within its pages. Read, apply what you learn and be blessed!

Selwyn Stevens, Ph.D.; D.Min.
President: Jubilee Resources International Inc.
Wellington, New Zealand

The 2 Minute Miracle of Blessing

The 2 Minute Miracle of Blessing

Releasing God's Power Through Your Thoughts, Words and Actions

REVISED & EXPANDED EDITION

with Study Guide

M. Lynn Reddick, Ph.D.

Cover design by Greg Reddick

ISBN: 978-0-9983060-0-1
ISBN: 978-0-9983060-1-8 (eBook)

Printed in the United States of America

Dedicated to my wife
Linda A. Reddick
God's gift to this generation

.

Contents

Foreword

By Jim Rutz

THE SPOKEN BLESSING is the biggest power ever lost! In Old Testament times, it was more common, but nowadays we just say, "I'll pray for ya'."

Lynn Reddick knows how to speak things into existence! And he does it almost every day. He has brought the power of the spoken blessing back to thousands of people, teaching them how to transform lives by speaking blessings.

In this book he shows how to change someone's life and destiny. And yes, it only takes about two minutes. People are astonished when they see the power and love of God in action as they bless others.

We feel this is definitely the easiest and fastest way to permanently erase a person's problems and bestow on them new power and strength they never had before.

Lynn is today's foremost authority on blessing. He and his wife Linda travel worldwide, training people in the practices explained in *The 2 Minute Miracle of Blessing.*

Introduction

YOU ARE ABOUT TO MAKE A DISCOVERY that can change your life. It is a hidden treasure so powerful you'll wonder how you lived without it.

If you have windburn on your face and thorns in your feet from running at break-neck speed searching for a better life, this book is for you. You won't have to face another day thinking, *what's the use?* or walking where negative feelings linger like the smell of fried fish.

The following pages will lead you past persistent obstacles, familiar detours and annoying delays. You will *finally* discover the key to unlock the storehouse of your blessings.

You'll learn how to release supernatural power by thinking and speaking *positive words or blessings* that change people. And, as strange as it may sound, this will change you, too.

What you think, speak and do—thoughts, words and actions—are like echoes. You receive back exactly what you give out—good or bad, positive or negative. It's not good luck or bad luck; it is the biblical principle of sowing and reaping.

I'll share part of my journey in the next section—a journey from a time and place where positive words or blessings were not often given; a place where you earned praise and approval for what you did, not for who you were.

Together, we can walk this path out of negative thinking and speaking into a world where God is real, miracles still happen, and life is worth living.

Really!

In The Beginning

(A Personal Statement)

WHERE I GREW UP, a blessing was used three ways: a blessing for mealtimes, a "bless you!" for sneezes and a "blessing out"[1] when someone had it out with you. A prayer, a wish and a scolding.

Years later, I saw another kind of blessing demonstrated at a mountain retreat in Colorado that changed my life. It happened around a supper table as one person told another how special they were and how God loved them. Though this exercise had the appearance of a religious ritual, something more was going on as handkerchiefs appeared around the table.

I thought, *what is happening?*

"This is what we call 'blessing,'" someone said, as if my question prompted a response.

Deep primal stirrings inside me, like a geyser ready to burst from an ancient underground cavern, increased as I left the table that evening.

Later that night, several childhood memories emerged from behind the curtain of unmet needs. How I wished *my* parents had looked me in the eyes just once and blessed me, told me they were proud of me, loved me, believed in me and my future! I felt their silence hobbled me emotionally.

It didn't take long to figure out that I had to do something with what I saw and felt around that "Table of Blessing." Would I continue the curse of silence by not blessing *my* family and those around me?

As we drove down the mountain the next morning, questions kept running through the streets of my mind.

When my wife Linda and I missed our flight the next morning, we found ourselves in a local café with our friends Jim Rutz and Dean Cozzens.

Answers began to emerge.

For 30 years, we taught and demonstrated small group dynamics using open sharing instead of lecture-type teaching. Jim captured this idea in his book, *The Open Church*, encouraging leaders to give everyone the opportunity to share something in meetings rather than one person doing all the talking.

"Jim," I asked, "why don't we plan one-day workshops showing people how to have open sharing and start small groups; maybe even open churches? And, we could learn more about the power of blessing and include that in the workshops."

Jim agreed and set into motion one-day workshops and three-day camps across the United States and into Canada.

Initially, we taught and demonstrated blessing only a few minutes during the first few workshops. Soon deep fundamental needs within people required more time for blessing one another.

We saw blessings restore the friendship of two women; save the marriage of a wife ready to call it quits and change the life of a teenager who was thinking about jumping off a bridge.

Surprising responses from these workshops began pouring in from across the country. A participant from Newark, New Jersey, said, "The second most important event of my life." In Elmira, New York: "This is a turning point in my life. I will never be the same!" A Minneapolis man commented: "I would have come 2,000 miles to hear this. There are millions who need this teaching." Randy in San Diego said, "Excuse me for using the words 'blown away' a lot, but it was powerful. Our lives are forever changed." And in Denver, Colorado, an older woman's comment: "This is what has been missing my entire life."

In 1998, Linda and I made the discovery that changed *our* lives and the lives of many people around us. After a year teaching and demonstrating the power of blessing through nationwide one-day workshops and three-day camps, we knew this was only the beginning of identifying inner needs.

Blessing releases a healing balm on emotional and spiritual wounds and in some cases, even physical sickness and disease.

THE 2 MINUTE MIRACLE IS BORN

We look for and talk about what we need the most. I need healing of deep ruts in my mental, emotional and spiritual landscape— furrows carved by negative thinking, critical judgments and religious condemnation.

Someone said that memory keeps an archive of moments. My depository contains some tarnished moments searching for healing— memories of withheld blessings that stir feelings of fear, guilt, resentment and inferiority.

I knew learning to give and receive blessings was a divine prescription for healing my inner self as well as medicine for other people struggling with some of the same issues.

Following our discovery of the power of blessing, it took five years to put thoughts and experiences in a book on blessing called, *The 2 Minute Miracle.* This became a bestseller in

New Zealand, and here in America, thousands of people basked in the afterglow of blessing workshops, many strangely moved by frequent miracles occurring when one person blessed another.

The response to *The 2 Minute Miracle* and increased interest in our workshops prompted the release of this Revised and Expanded Edition entitled, *The 2 Minute Miracle of Blessing*, with twice the information contained in the 2003 Edition.

We'll examine four ways a blessing is given: by thinking, at a distance, in writing and face-to-face.

First, blessings can be sent by thinking positive thoughts that affect us, things and people. Solomon said, "For as he thinks in his heart, so is he."[2] Thinking sends thought-waves cascading through the world around us—far and near—with powerful effect.[3] Have you ever thought of a long-lost friend and had them contact you suddenly?

Secondly, you'll see how blessings spoken at a distance are effective. For example, Balaam blessed the Hebrews coming into the Promise Land at a distance.[4] And, Jesus spoke distant healing to a centurion's servant.[5]

Writing is the third way blessings are expressed. Words coming through our eye-gate are digested in the mind and birth an emotional response. The Apostle Paul gave comfort and reassurance to churches in letters ending with a blessing.[6]

Finally, blessings given face-to-face convey love and goodwill through warmth expressed with eye contact and touch. Jesus blessed people face-to-face with words of healing[7] and abundant life.[8]

THE RIPPLE EFFECT

Regardless of the way a blessing is given, you will see the powerful effect they have in real-life stories.

As you read this book, you might wonder why Linda and I have experienced so many phenomenal things. *Could things like this ever happen to me?* You might ask.

If you want exciting things to happen to you, put yourself in places where they can. These "places" are where *learning to bless* will take you. It's the law of sowing and reaping. Whether with thoughts, words or actions, we receive what we give. The New Testament plainly states, "A man reaps what he sows."[9] This spiritual principle appears in many world religions.[10]

As you journey through the following pages, you'll be inspired to unlock the door of *your* storehouse of blessings by blessing God, people, things and yourself—not once or twice, but regularly.

Think of the *ripple effect* as a drop of water plops in a pool. Small waves ruffle the surface, changing its shape. This mental picture captures the effect blessings have—changing moods, impacting people and cascading through the environment.

Take time to notice the ripples a blessing leaves in its wake. This is such an exhilarating experience you'll wonder how you lived without it.

Never pay back one wrong with another,
or an angry word with another one;
Instead, pay back with a blessing.
This is what you are called to do,
so that you inherit [obtain] a blessing yourself.
1 Peter 3:9, *The Jerusalem Bible*

1

Why Can't I Just Forgive?
(Isn't That Enough?)

WHEN I MET CHUCK he seemed to be climbing the ladder of success rapidly. And why not? His good looks and great personality endeared him to others, and he excelled as a gifted singer, baseball player and college student.

He was close to his family, especially his larger-than-life grandfather who was the center of his life from early childhood. This man didn't mince words, however, especially in voicing his expectations of his grandson.

Over the period of a few weeks in his freshman year, several unusual events converged on Chuck at one time. He scored badly on a college exam, quit a part-time job and decided against a professional baseball career. This news reached his grandfather the same weekend Chuck dropped by for a visit.

A barrage of harsh criticism met Chuck at the

door, more intense than anything before. Repeatedly, his grandfather demeaned him, told him he was no good and that he would never amount to anything. These words took root in Chuck's mind and emotions. After his grandfather died unexpectedly a few weeks later, they began to grow.

Over time these word-curses would alter Chuck's identity (who he was) and destiny (where he'd go). Laughter was the first to leave, followed by his interest in music, then his involvement in the local church. After dropping out of college, he began to vacillate from job to job, and years later, from wife to wife. Buried hurts produced a cursed life by a grandfather whom Chuck couldn't forgive.

BURIED HURTS AND EMOTIONAL SCARS

Our highly developed central nervous system makes us especially vulnerable to hurtful words and actions. Given this propensity for emotional injury—or soul wounds—combined with our fallen nature, it's not surprising that we tend to *nurse* a hurt by mental brooding, *rehearse* the hurt with other people, or *curse* the hurt through blame rather than *reverse* the hurt by forgiving.

An emotional quagmire soon develops:

An *insult* leads to *injury* which naturally stirs *anger* (conscious or unconscious), resulting in a *refusal to forgive.* This breeds *resentment or hate* which produces a *curse* (physical, emotional, and spiritual harm) on the person's life.

The mind can't feel pain, so emotional hurts pass on to the body for either resolution or burial. Don't think, however, that burial means gone-for-good. Buried hurts become planted in the soil of the subconscious and sprout in bodily symptoms. In other words, *the body reveals what the mind conceals.*

A good analogy of this is a childhood experience I had on our farm in Georgia. I attempted a short cut in my pea-planting chores one afternoon by burying a whole bucket of peas at the end of a row. What I thought was buried came back to haunt me about a week later—in a big way.

When someone is emotionally hurt and withholds forgiveness, resentment begins to germinate deep within like buried seeds. Hate soon emerges in one form or another.

The Bible doesn't distinguish between resentment and hate because of the fine line separating them. Hate is such an intensive, destructive emotion that the Bible equates it with murder.[1]

Resentment becomes a buried seed that produces the fruit of bitterness, depression and physical illness, often disguising itself in the clothes of justification: "I have the right to feel this way." However, resentment or hate becomes a curse in four areas:

- Physically, it can contribute to illnesses such as stomach ulcers, arthritis and some types of headaches, skin rashes and cancers.
- Emotionally, it will poison the mind and defile the mouth.
- Socially, it can destroy our closest friendships, including those with spouse and children.
- Spiritually, it will destroy our relationship with God.

The misery and torment caused by hate are characteristic of evil in the world, especially Satan who seeks to inflict misery on everything God creates. Hate is so destructive that God created hell to isolate Satan and hate in the future.[2]

Everyone who allows hate to take root and rule their lives is destined for this abyss of unimaginable torment.

We've all been insulted by someone and felt the stirrings of anger—and at that moment we made a decision, conscious or unconscious within ourselves. We could either harbor that insult or redirect the energy in a positive way.

If we refuse to forgive, resentment can grow into hate and produce curses which help shape a person's identity and destiny as in the case of Chuck.

DRIVE-BY BLESSINGS

Ideally, no one can insult us unless we allow those words to affect us. However, most people don't live in this realm of reality.

What happens when an insult causes emotional injury and stirs anger? A soul-wound brings us to moments of decision. Do we forgive or do we withhold forgiveness? Either decision determines our long-term physical, emotional and spiritual health.

If the negative effects of unforgiving are so consequential, why doesn't everyone choose to forgive? Human nature and alienation from God are major barriers. After evil entered the human experience, responding with eye-for-eye and tooth-for-tooth is easier than forgiving.

People reconnected to God through Jesus Christ have an advantage in decisive moments because the indwelling Holy Spirit helps "in our weakness."[3] However, working through negative feelings is another matter as I discovered a few years ago when the Lord nudged Linda and me to go to Atlanta and start a new church.

The Spirit of God directed us to a financially depressed area where we connected with a couple who helped us start the new church. Over the next two years they became our best friends.

One Saturday, we had what I thought was a minor disagreement about the direction the church should take. The following day as the church family gathered for singing and open sharing, my best friend chose to embarrass me before the congregation. His verbal hand grenade exploded in my face and splattered emotional blood everywhere.

In the midst of the hullabaloo, the Lord spoke to my inner self:

> *Forget the hurt. Forgive the man.*
> *But Lord, He didn't tell the whole story.*
> *Forget the hurt. Forgive the man.*
> *But Lord . . .*

Forgiving during times of increase was easier than times of decrease as the congregation scattered like a flock of birds. What a struggle choosing to forgive in the face of what felt like utter betrayal on the one hand and financial disaster on the other as church collections fell to nearly zero! It was a Humpty Dumpty story where things couldn't be put back together again.

After weeks of befuddled feelings of anger and resentment, I knew what had to be done. In the same community where Truett Cathy invented the chicken sandwich, perhaps I invented the drive-by blessing.

I decided to drive by my ex-friend's house a distance off the highway and speak forgiveness— from the road.

I'd drive by with window rolled down, stick my hand out and holler, "I forgive you and bless you."

It might have sounded good, but I was lying!

Didn't mean a word I said!

But I knew if I continued saying what was needed, one day I'd *really* mean it.

I didn't expect this drive-by pardon to mend our relationship. But I did know that sitting on a lot of pent up frustration and anger could either be held in or released. I needed to forgive this man because of the devastating effects of negative feelings festering inside like a malignant cancer.

One year later, the man who pulled the shenanigan in front of our congregation phoned to ask forgiveness for the way he acted.

A result of my drive-by blessings?

Deep wounds produce emotional scars which itch at times. After three years, thinking I had completely worked through any hurt feelings, I saw a man at a distance in a parking lot that closely resembled the betrayer. When a cold emotional chill swept over me like an icy North Pole wind, I knew there was more buried hurt within.

Yes, Lord. I understand. Keep forgiving.

Four years after the verbal ambush, I dropped by the local Home Depot and headed down an aisle near the back of the warehouse.

The only two shoppers at the far end didn't notice me approaching at first, but as I got within 30 feet their heads raised.

For the first time in four years, our eyes met. The hair on the back of my neck didn't bristle. Nothing coiled up inside my chest.

As I got closer an almost supernatural peace seemed to cover me like a mantle.

Brushing aside his outstretched hand in my direction, I gave him our customary warm hug. Then I warmly greeted his wife, just like old times.

As I walked outside the building, a surge of emotions caught me by surprise. It was like walking out of a state penitentiary, released from a very long confinement.

YES! YES!

My shouts of joy turned heads and slowed traffic in the parking lot.

This warehouse reunion didn't restore our friendship, but for me, it demonstrated God's power to *finally* heal my soul wounds.

FORGIVE *AND* BLESS

It began in Jerusalem as the Jews gathered for an eight-day celebration of Passover, Unleavened Bread, and Firstfruits. These festive holidays brought a well-known itinerant prophet-healer and his disciples to the city.

Gathering in an upstairs room, this widely acclaimed Messiah ate the ancient Passover meal with twelve of his followers. They remembered the mighty acts of God in Egypt when death swept over that nation, killing the firstborn of every man and animal but passing over Hebrew families.

All went well at the supper table until Jesus began speaking strange words about betrayal, blood, suffering and death. The following three-day Jerusalem nightmare darkened all Messianic hopes when his disciples saw their carpenter friend hanging lifeless between two criminals.

Grief spread like a plague across Jerusalem, killing all hope of overthrowing Roman oppression or crowning the long-awaited Messiah.

Despondency and fear drove the remaining eleven men into a locked dining room out of harm's way from Jewish authorities. Imagine the shock when a ghost-like figure, passing through a wall, stood in front of them and said,

"Shalom!" By now, this distressed group needed peace.

They were flabbergasted that their friend Jesus was *alive!* Disbelief slowly lifted as sorrow became joy and despair gave way to hope. Soon, fearful cowards would become courageous power teams throughout the known world.

But not without a price.

It wasn't long before severe persecution broke out. What should a person do in the face of such hostilities? Pay back by trying to get even?

Peter wrote encouraging words to those who were walking through pain, oppression and suffering. He charted a different course for these early believers—and us—by suggesting that we pay back a wrong deed or an angry word with blessings.

Never pay back one wrong with another,
or an angry word with another one;
instead, pay back with a blessing.
This is what you are called to do,
so that you inherit a blessing yourself.[4]

But, here's the rub. Before we can sincerely bless someone, we must forgive them of any emotional wounds they might have caused. This principle can be traced back 3,000 years to the Proverbs of a king named Solomon. "If a man pays back evil for good, evil will never leave his house."[5] "Do not say, 'I'll pay back for this wrong!' Wait for the Lord, and he will deliver you."[6]

These axioms of revenge, planted in the soil of human history, sprouted 1,000 years later and developed into major life principles of forgiveness by Jesus. He taught that if we hold anything against anyone, we must forgive them so we will be forgiven by God.[7]

We must forgive so *we* will be forgiven.

If we choose to forgive—not based on how we feel about the person or what was said, but on our *decision* to take no offense—an emotional timeline of forgiveness unfolds this way:

An *insult* leads to *injury* which naturally
stirs *anger* and brings us to a decision.
Forgiveness extends *acceptance and love*
that brings *blessings.*

Although we can initiate forgiveness with a decision, God has to work within us to heal our soul wounds and stir love and acceptance for the offender. What we initiate with a decision He cultivates by His Spirit to bring us to the point of heartfelt forgiveness.

Forgiving and blessing open the door to *our* blessings.

Perhaps this is why these empowered believers "turned the world upside down,"[8] at least for the first 200 years. They learned to forgive and speak blessings instead of begrudging curses. Forgiving *and* blessing others released God's hand of blessings in their lives.

Quite a life-principle as Mike discovered one day!

It started out like any other Sunday as our church family gathered to worship. That particular morning I spoke on the power of forgiving, urging everyone to replace hurt and resentment with spoken blessings.

Mike was among the first to request help at the end of the meeting. A couple took him aside to discuss his needs. I walked over just in time to hear Mike tell how he felt discarded all of his life. Not only did his mother give him away at birth, she never contacted him one time.

For 34 years, he lived without any knowledge of his mother, where she was or if she was alive. Rejection, inferiority, guilt and resentment plagued his life. A loving wife and two children didn't ease the pain of feeling worthless.

The counseling couple discussed the need to speak forgiveness to his absent mother. They placed an empty chair in front of Mike.

"Tell your mother how you feel," they said.

Mike began speaking from his heart. "Mom, I forgive you for giving me away. But I'm so lonely. If I could just hear your voice, feel your touch, know that you love me. I bless you as my mother and ask God to release you from guilt and condemnation."

There was a knock at my office door the next morning.

It was Mike.

"I forgave and blessed my mother yesterday," he said, "not only at the end of our church meeting but all afternoon. You'll never believe what happened during supper last night."

"What happened?" I asked.

"The phone rang. It was my mother!"

He paused for a moment overcome with emotion. Then he said, "She asked me to forgive her!"

This story is unimaginable but true. It demonstrates the power of forgiving *and* blessing even at a distance. (Mike's mother phoned from 2,000 miles away!)

NUTS, BOLTS AND WASHERS

After high school graduation I spent the summer in my hometown of Portal working at the recreational department, a job paying an astonishing $100 per week. Not much today, but for an 18-year-old back then, it was quite a lot.

Problem was, Larry, who wrote my weekly checks, overlooked paying me the last $100. I brooded over this incident so much that my hurt hardened into resentment. To further compound the problem, I had to pass his house to get almost anywhere from mine. Even going to college didn't help much. Home on weekends, I'd drive by Larry's house only to experience an onslaught of negative thoughts and feelings. Thoughts of revenge flooding my mind kept hitting the wall of forgiveness.

I sensed the Lord saying to me, *forget the $100; forgive and bless the man*—so often that emotional peace begged me to obey.

When feelings of resentment did stir, I'd tell myself that I decided to forgive and bless Larry. I would quietly speak as if he was standing near, "I forgive and bless you. May God bless you and forgive me."

Eventually, I *forgot* the $100.

When I became president of a Christian organization in Colorado, office furnishings were moved from Colorado Springs and stored near my home in Georgia until a new office location was determined.

A few months later, sitting in my truck in the middle of my hometown, I looked at a vacant building directly in front of me. I heard the words: *That is the building.*

A phone call arranged the meeting with the owners. I explained the vision and ministry Linda and I were called to do.

"I am here to ask you to give our organization that building," I said. "We don't want to buy it or rent it. We're asking you to give it to us."

Questions followed, including one of mine.

"Why hasn't the building been rented for several years?"

I was told that there were about 75 tons of nuts, bolts and washers in the building, and the owners didn't know what to do with them.

"Why don't you put them in small bags and sell them to local farmers at a cut-rate price," I suggested.

Two weeks passed before we heard from the owners.

"Lynn, we've reached a decision. We want to give your organization the building."

In four weeks all of the nuts, bolts and washers had been sold.

Quite a feat in itself.

I was driving back through Portal from the attorney's office with the property deed. As I pulled out of town, suddenly, I heard a voice inside me, *Remember the $100."*

These words were so real I pulled off onto the shoulder of the highway. I sat there a few moments trying to figure out what the words meant that sent shockwaves through my head.

I looked over to my right and realized I was sitting in front of a familiar house—the house of Larry Smith who, 40 years earlier, never paid me that last $100!

Larry and Joann Smith had just given us the $100,000 building in the middle of town—one that would become the headquarters of our ministry.

The Lord's presence filled the truck cab as tears welled up in my eyes. I heard these inaudible words:

Because you forgave and learned to bless the man, today, I have taken that $100 and turned it into $100,000.

This incident is about more than nuts, bolts and washers. It's about struggling to forgive and learning to speak blessings in place of brooding resentment. It's about the God of provision who is looking for people He can bless and create a ripple effect in other people.

That's the reason we can't just forgive someone. Peter says that we must pay back those who hurt us with blessings. This, he says, "is what we are called to do."⁹

Blessing initiates or deepens the process of forgiving in us. It's a guard against hurt feelings hiding in a dark corner of our lives. As we speak blessings to our offender, in person or at a distance, light exposes any hidden insincerity in us.

We don't just think forgiveness; we *speak* forgiveness with blessings until emotional knots are loosened and freedom comes both to us and our offender.

In the next chapter you'll discover what blessing is, as well as the source. You'll be awed by the powerful, mysterious and supernatural impact spoken blessings have upon people and things—often in a matter of minutes.

The Ripple Effect

A Letter from Rome

Blessing Mends a Marriage

My husband and I have been married for 30 years. Recently we hit a "dry spell" where some hurtful words were spoken which led to thoughts of separation. We were already in the process of separating emotionally, just not physically. We loved each other—just lost our way for a spell.

We were searching for something more in each other—in the Lord as well. Some of our friends had encouraged us to seek counseling of which I would have no part.

Your Blessing Workshop on Saturday morning changed our marriage forever! Saved us lots of money in counseling! I will never forget the presence of God in that room EVER.

As my husband and I stood before you and Linda, it seemed as if we were the only ones in the room. I don't quite remember all the words spoken by my husband. I do remember feeling that HEALING was taking place, as if the Lord erased the "mess" we had created. We spoke blessings to each other and then sat down in a "wow" state of mind.

2

Paper Blessings & More

EVENTS OF A SINGLE DAY shaped the lives of Mark and his classmates. Schoolteacher Helen Morsla tells the story:

He was in a third-grade class I taught at Saint Mary's School in Morris, Minnesota. All thirty-four students were dear to me, but Mark Eklund was one in a million. Very neat in appearance, he had that happy-to-be-alive attitude that made even his occasional mischievousness delightful. Mark talked incessantly. I had to remind him again and again that talking without permission was not acceptable. What impressed me so much, though, was his sincere response every time I had to correct him for misbehaving: "Thank you for correcting me, Sister!"

I didn't know what to make of it at first, but before long I became accustomed to hearing it many times a day.

One morning my patience was growing thin when Mark talked once too often, and then I made a novice-teacher's mistake. I looked at Mark and said, "If you say one more word, I am going to tape your mouth shut!"

It wasn't ten seconds later when Chuck blurted out, "Mark is talking again." I hadn't asked any of the students to help me watch Mark, but since I had stated the punishment in front of the class, I had to act on it.

I remember the scene as if it had occurred this morning. I walked to my desk, very deliberately opened my drawer and took out a roll of masking tape. Without saying a word, I proceeded to Mark's desk, tore off two pieces of tape and made a big X with them over his mouth. I then returned to the front of the room.

As I glanced at Mark to see how he was doing, he winked at me. That did it! I started laughing. The class cheered as I walked back to Mark's desk, removed the tape, and shrugged my shoulders. His first words were, "Thank you for correcting me, Sister."

At the end of the year, I was asked to teach junior-high math. The years flew by, and before I knew it Mark was in my classroom again. He was more handsome than ever and just as polite. Since he had to listen carefully to my instruction in the "new math," he did not talk as much in ninth grade as he had in the third.

One Friday, things just didn't feel right. We had worked hard on a new concept all week, and I sensed that the students were frowning, frustrated with themselves, and edgy with one another. I had to stop this crankiness before it got out of hand. So I asked them to list the names of the other students in the room on two sheets of paper, leaving a space between each name. Then I told them to think of the nicest thing they could say about each of their classmates and write it down. They took the remainder of the class period to finish their assignment.

As the students left the room, each one handed me their paper. Mark said, "Thank you for teaching me, Sister. Have a good weekend."

That Saturday, I wrote down the name of each student on a separate sheet of paper, and I listed what everyone else had said about that individual. On Monday I gave each student his or her list. Before long, the entire class was smiling.

"Really?" I heard whispered.

"I never knew that meant anything to anyone!"

"I didn't know others liked me so much."

No one ever mentioned those papers in class again. I never knew if they discussed them after class or with their parents, but it didn't matter. The exercise had accomplished its purpose. The students were happy with themselves and one another again.

That group of students moved on. Several years later after I returned from vacation, my parents met me at the airport. As we were driving home, Mother asked me the usual questions about the trip, the weather, my experiences in general. There was a lull in the conversation. Mother gave Dad a sideways glance and simply said, "Dad?" My father cleared his throat as he usually did before saying something important.

"The Eklunds called last night," he began.

"Really?" I said. "I haven't heard from them in years. I wonder how Mark is."

Dad responded quietly. "Mark was killed in Vietnam," he said. "The funeral is tomorrow, and his parents would like it if you could attend."

To this day I can still point to the exact spot on I-494 where Dad told me about Mark.

I had never seen a serviceman in a military coffin before. Mark looked so handsome, so mature. All I could think at that moment was, *Mark, I would give all the masking tape in the world if only you would talk to me.*

The church was packed with Mark's friends. Chuck's sister sang "The Battle Hymn of the Republic." Why did it have to rain on the day of the funeral? It was difficult enough at the graveside. The priest said the usual prayers, and the bugler played taps. One by one those who loved Mark took a last walk by the coffin and sprinkled it with holy water.

I was the last one to bless the coffin. As I stood there, one of the soldiers who acted as pallbearer came up to me. "Were you Mark's math teacher?" he asked. I nodded as I continued to stare at the coffin.

"Mark talked about you a lot," he said.

After the funeral, most of Mark's former classmates headed to Chuck's farmhouse for lunch. Mark's mother and father were there, obviously waiting for me. "We want to show you something," his father said, taking a wallet out of his pocket. "They found this on Mark when he was killed. We thought you might recognize it."

Opening the billfold, he carefully removed two worn pieces of notebook paper that had obviously been taped, folded and refolded many times. I knew without looking that the papers were the ones on which I had listed all the good things each of Mark's classmates had said about him.

"Thank you so much for doing that," Mark's mother said. "As you can see, Mark treasured it."

Mark's classmates started to gather around us. Charlie smiled rather sheepishly and said, "I still have my list. It's in the top drawer of my desk at home."

Chuck's wife said, "Chuck asked me to put his in our wedding album."

Then Vickie, another classmate, reached into her pocketbook, took out her wallet and showed her worn and frazzled list to the group. "I carry this with me at all times," Vicki said without batting an eyelash. "I think we all saved our lists."

That's when I finally sat down and cried. I cried for Mark and for all his friends who would never see him again.

If affirmations on paper have such impact, imagine the powerful effect words have, not written once, but spoken repeatedly!

THE SOURCE

The word *bless* derives its meaning from Old and New Testament words *barak* and *eulogeo* respectively. While both have the meaning "to pronounce blessed," *barak* means to convey a gift with a powerful utterance as God did over His creation. *Eulogeo,* from which we get the word "eulogy," means to speak well of (*eu,* "well," *logos,* "a word"), cause to benefit from material things[1] and to make happy and prosperous.[2]

The Amplified Bible expands the meaning of blessing to include "welfare, happiness and protection."[3] Speaking blessings can release God's power, goodness, favor and protection. Each of Paul's letter closes with a blessing upon both hearers and readers.

God first spoke blessings over His creation by releasing His power and purpose in both animals and people: "Be fruitful and increase in number."[4] This set the tone of God's favor toward creation as a loving Father who desired to pour out His love and favor upon us. Later, He sent His one-of-a-kind Son to show everyone His goodness and mercy. From the beginning of creation, He revealed His desire to bless.

RELEASE THE FLOW

Sneeze in Israel, they say, "To your health." Germans say, "Good health." Where English is spoken it is, "God Bless you." All these sneeze responses mean the same: "I see by your sneeze that you may be getting sick. I bless you with good health."

While this biblical concept acknowledges God as the source of blessings, *we* release His power, goodness, favor and protection by speaking blessings into other people's lives. Our authority to bless can be seen in Jesus' instructions to "let *your* peace rest upon it" [home].[5]

One of the best-known examples of a father's blessing is found in Genesis 27 where Isaac's blessing for his son, Jacob, consists of the power of life, fertility and prosperity. Later, the New Testament included the idea of well-being and happiness.

When we bless, something living and active is released in the invisible world around us that brings positive benefits to someone. Through blessings God can touch and stir something within the person that might have been spoken or stirred previously.

Linda and I were teaching in a three-night meeting a few years ago. She received a strong impression that a middle-aged businessman present was running from God's call on his life. Later in the meeting Linda blessed him as a man of God with a divine call.

"Wasn't there a time when you felt God wanted you to be a pastor?" she asked.

"Absolutely not! God has never given me such an impression," he said, and returned to his seat.

I was a bit apprehensive the second night when the same man returned to the meeting. As we started, he lifted his hand and asked to address the group.

"When Linda blessed me as a man called by God, I thought that was absurd. But last night I dreamed I was sitting in a clump of trees behind my house reading my Bible. I felt like the Lord spoke to my heart and called me to be a pastor. When I woke up, I remembered that actually happened when I was eight years old. But I didn't want anything to do with church or God, so I forgot the experience. I guess I buried it in my subconscious. Last night, Linda's blessing stirred something deep within me that I had suppressed all these years."

CALLED TO BLESS

The story of Adam and Eve depicts man's inborn disconnect from God. It is our story of alienation from the Creator.

The mission of Jesus was to restore this connection between Divine Spirit (God) and human spirit (us). Jesus' sinless life, death and resurrection were accepted by Father God as a substitute for our sin-debt. As we accept Jesus Christ as our Savior, the Holy Spirit begins to flow through us with spiritual gifts and blessings.

Many of God's blessings are conditionally based on our obedience rather than being gift certificates. These blessings hover over us and will "overtake us" *if* we obey God.[6] As our Creator and Father, He knows what is needed if each one of us is to reach full potential and have joy-filled lives.

The Bible is intended as our guide to abundant living, not a rule book of burdensome "thou shalt" and "thou shalt not." Put another way, obeying God brings blessings whereas disobedience unleashes curses.[7] However, there are instances when God blesses and promises to bless simply because He *wants* to bless, not because we have any merit or are required to do something.

Jacob began the struggle with his twin brother in the womb, bargained for the birthright with food and gained his father's blessing by deception. Yet, through the fascinating interplay between fate and free will, destiny and choice, Jacob still received both parental blessings and those of God.

Only God knows the thoughts and motives of each person. He alone decides which blessings to freely give and which come with a condition.

One reason God blesses us is so we, in turn, can bless other people, things and our surroundings. God's life-energy is released in the world thorough our blessings in a ripple effect.

This call to bless has its roots in the ancient tribe of Levi who served as priests in their nation "to pronounce blessings in his [God's] name."[8]

Later, Jesus expanded this call to bless to include everyone who has been put back right with God, making *every* Christian a priest invested with the authority and power to bless in Christ's name.[9]

OPEN EYE BLESSING

One of the greatest gifts one person can give another is to speak blessings into his or her life. When Rebekah's family sent her away to marry Isaac, they blessed her and said, "Our sister, may you increase to thousands upon thousands; may your offspring possess the gates of their enemies."[10]

With this prophetic blessing Rebekah became the dynamic person to whom God revealed His plan to work through Jacob rather than Esau. Rebekah set in motion events to see that this plan was properly carried out.

Most traditional blessings have been given as prayers. Although we might assume the blessing of Aaron and those of Paul were prayers, there are no indications these were given in a closed-eye manner.

While blessings can be used as prayers, they are more effectively given face-to-face in many situations. In prayer blessings, we speak *to God* for someone. In face-to-face blessings, we speak to someone *for God*.

Face-to-face blessings are effective because the face expresses inward thoughts and feelings. Blessing in this way allows us to communicate feelings much better.

Suppose you find yourself in the breakfast line of a crowded Chick-fil-A, standing behind a grumpy old man glaring at his food tray. He shakes his head like it's barely connected to the rest of his body and complains to the server behind the counter.

"This is NOT what I ordered," he snaps. "I want a Bacon, Egg & Cheese Biscuit. You gave me a Sausage, Egg & Cheese Biscuit. This stupid mistake makes me think it's your first day on the job!"

The young girl stares at the tray, overwhelmed by the insults hurled over the counter. Several people behind you clear their throats as the old man snatches his tray and disappears in the crowd.

"May...May I, I take your order?" she says, still stunned by the lingering insult.

Suppose you decide to respond with a blessing. There are two ways to do this: the closed eye blessing or the open eye blessing.

First, you see her name is Sue, so you say, "Sue, I want to bless you." You close your eyes and say, "Father, I ask you to heal Sue's hurts and bless her today in Jesus' name. Amen."

How do you think this would make her feel? What about the manager who is now standing near her? What about the reaction of the people behind you?

A little religious and embarrassing would you say?

Now, consider the open eye blessing. You look at her and say, "Sue, those words really hurt don't they? If you were my daughter, I'd be proud of you for getting up early to come to work. Thank you for serving me."

You decide which kind of blessing fits this situation best. Remember, you're not speaking to God for the young woman. You're speaking to her for God—saying what He might say.

In a workshop, Jim stood behind his seated wife, Marcia, placed his hands on her shoulders and began blessing her. While the words were intimate, the connection was not. I interrupted and asked Jim to get in front of Marcia, take her hands, look her in the eyes and continue. Immediately, he saw the greater emotional impact his words had, especially as tears of joy rolled down her cheeks.

THE AUTHORITY

It's easy to understand why Helen Morsla's third grade class wrote blessings to fellow classmates. They were told to do so. You saw how written blessings shared with other students did the trick. Love and acceptance were expressed and treasured for years—because someone gave the students instruction and authority.

This is similar to our authority and command to speak blessings *for* God. Historically, speaking for God has been reserved for the clergy class. Go to the priest, rabbi or pastor to get a word from God. But what if you can learn to hear the inner voice of the Holy Spirit? What if you can learn to speak His love and life into other people?

Christ's authority is found in eight scriptures, allowing *any Christian* to look someone in the eyes and bless them—saying things for their strengthening, encouraging and comfort.[11]

1. We have His *call or command* to bless.[12]
2. We have His *example* to bless.[13]
3. We have His *mind* to bless.[14]
4. We have His *nature* to bless.[15]
5. We have His *power* to bless.[16]
6. We have His *Spirit* to bless.[17]
7. We have His *authority as priests* to bless.[18]
8. We have His *commission as ambassadors* to bless.[19]

BLESS IN FOUR AREAS

Christ has given people authority to bless in

four areas or realms to reveal His Kingdom on Earth: spiritual realm (God),[20] material realm (things),[21] social realm (people),[22] and personal realm (ourselves).[23]

Blessing God has been the primary focus of the Jewish and Christian communities for centuries. This has been almost the exclusive use of blessing, because God deserves our first and highest praise. This recognition of God should lead us to bless things, people and ourselves because these are God's creations. He has not only given us the authority to bless, *He has commanded us to bless* as seen in the above scriptures.

Speaking to things demonstrates our dominion in the material realm. One thinks of Elijah speaking to the sky,[24] the Hebrews shouting to the walls of Jericho,[25] and Jesus speaking to a fig tree[26] and wind.[27] These biblical examples can't be easily dismissed because they are in the past and no longer apply to us today.

Our authority to speak to and bless things around us demonstrates our God-given dominion over His creation. It's not our authority that's lacking. It's our faith—faith to speak words that release God's power. God said to Moses, "Speak to that rock before their eyes and it will pour out its water."[28]

My friend, Sapp Lee, lives a few miles down the road. He learned about faith some years back and told me his story, a story that will leave permanent stretch marks on your religious skin.

Sapp stood looking over 1,000 acres of soybeans heavily infested with armyworms, 1 ½-inch-long critters that move across fields—like an army, chopping away with lightning speed. In just one or two days entire fields could be completely destroyed by these ferocious eaters.

He knew it would take an airplane to get his 56 fields sprayed in time to prevent total devastation. With no money to hire a pilot or buy chemicals, he was still reeling from earlier crop failures that left him $950,000 in debt and no way to borrow more money. This Rocky Ford, Georgia, farmer was broke and desperate!

On Wednesday he waded through waist-high soybeans, shaking bushes and watching armyworms cover the ground under his feet. Earlier that morning he sensed the Holy Spirit telling him to rebuke the armyworms, speak blessings over his crop and nail printed scripture verses from Deuteronomy and Malachi on fence posts and several utility poles across the fields:

> All these blessings will come on you and accompany you if you obey the LORD your God: You will be blessed in the city and blessed in the country. The fruit of your womb will be blessed, and the crops of your hand.[29]

And I will rebuke the devourer for your sakes, so that he will not destroy the fruit of your ground, nor shall the vine fail to bear fruit for you in the field, says the LORD of hosts.[30]

He was willing to try anything. So, nail, rebuke and bless he did. Climbing back in his old farm truck, peace began to settle on him unlike anything he's experienced before. But, what seemed like peace could be numbness at the thought of losing 1,000 acres of soybeans and going bankrupt.

Or, maybe God *was* up to something.

He took one last glance in his rear view mirror as he kicked up dust down the dirt road toward home.

Sapp was in Statesboro on Thursday when he overheard several farmers complaining about their heavy infestation of armyworms. Rather than enter into conversation he crawled back into his truck and left. Did he really hear God? Was it his imagination? Nail scripture verses on poles across the fields? Rebuke the worms? Bless the soybeans? Who'd ever heard of such?

But, he did what he thought he heard on Wednesday.

It wasn't until Friday that Sapp finally sent two farmhands to inspect the soybeans. Yep! Didn't or couldn't go himself; just send ole Leon and Henry. Let them inspect the fields, shake the bushes, and report back.

A few weeks earlier these two farmhands reported something that caused head scratching in the Rocky Ford community. There was enough diesel fuel left to fill his tractor tank one last time—enough to plow about half a day. Problem was they needed three days to finish plowing all the fields. *That one tank of fuel lasted three full days!*

Whatever miracle of increase happened in the tractor tank, Sapp desperately needed another Divine intervention in his soybeans. All day Friday, Leon and Henry walked over 56 fields, shaking bushes and peering under leaves.

Early Saturday morning the armyworm detectives told Sapp what they found: *On 1,000 acres they found only three armyworms!* "Don't know what happened to all those worms, Mr. Sapp," they said, "but they just weren't there!"

And, the fields remained worm-free for the rest of the season, producing what Sapp said was "the best soybean crop I ever had."

(Dear reader, you might want to pause a moment, take a deep breath and ponder one of the biggest miracles that ever happened in Screven County, Georgia).

Why would God command us to bless Him, things, people and ourselves? Could it be that blessing helps acknowledge Him as Creator and

Lord of everything and everyone? Could it be that blessing keeps us thinking and speaking positive thoughts to guard against negative, critical thinking and speaking? Could it be that blessing guards our hearts against evil intrusions?

Love flows thorough us in a look, a word and a touch. Think about your dog waiting at the door for a blessing when you come home—a look (recognition), a word ("Hi Cleo") and a touch (pat on the head).

The energy of love flowing through us ripples through everything and everyone far and near.

THE RIPPLE EFFECT

A Written Blessing

This blessing was written for our grand-daughter Sarah at Christmas.

From the moment you were born, we knew you would be an extraordinary person. Now, fourteen years down the road of life, you are:
- adventurous (attempting to walk two miles to our house as a two-year old),
- artistic (capturing and releasing such awesome ideas on paper),
- ambitious (expressing inner stirrings through music—singing and playing the guitar).

It is not coincidental that your name is Sarah which means, *princess, royalty*. It's no wonder you are known for your vibrant personality, inner and outer beauty, deep devotion to God, outstanding talent and abilities, and popularity among your peers.

We are proud of who you are and where you're going in life. It is a joy and honor to call you our granddaughter.

A Surprise Blessing

Donald was laying water and sewer pipes in our cottage basement while I was under the hot tub making wiring connections. I sensed the Lord nudging me to give Donald a blessing.

Oh, no! Not now, I thought. *I'm real busy and kinda pinned under this tub. How about later?*

The Familiar Voice inside me seemed rather persistent—real persistent!

Okay; okay!

I slid from under the tub, went to the front porch and called, "Donald, I need to see you.

He climbed the steps brushing dirt and grime from his face, arms and work clothes. "What do you want?" he asked.

"I believe I need to give you a blessing.

"A what?" he asked.

"A blessing; God wants to say something to you in a blessing."

At this point I didn't have a clue what that was, but I knew as I began, the right words would come.

I placed both hands on his tall shoulders, looked him in the eyes: "Donald, the Lord says" ... and words of blessing began to flow.

Son, I have placed you as head of your family to lead them in My paths and walk with Me. You have given this place of leadership to your son. Take it back.

"That's it," I said. "Let's go back to work."

Two days later, I was doing a bit of grungy cleanup around our Ministry Center while the staff was away. Dressed in work boots, blue jeans and denim shirt, I caught sight of a long, black Lincoln car easing around the back of the building—and around our small farming town—that was NOT a common sight.

The muscular driver, donning a coat-and-tie, stepped through the back door as I turned off the vacuum cleaner.

"Where is Lynn Reddick?" he asked with a daunting look on his face.

We don't usually have the Mafia around our small town but the scene fit the movies: a herculean front man checking out the situation before the "Boss" entered the room to do business.

I hesitated a bit to calculate my next move, since he stood between me and the exit.

'Where is Lynn Reddick?'" He asked again with a bit more directness in his voice.

I have no idea where he is, but I'll tell him you dropped by, I thought.

Finally I heard myself say, "I am Lynn Reddick,"

At that precise moment the "Boss" came through the back door and glanced at his chauffeur who stepped aside. This man stood no more than a foot in front of me for several moments before speaking.

Perspiration running down my cheeks was not just from vacuuming!

He cleared his throat and poised a moment longer. "What did you say to my Dad?" he asked with a quivering voice and moistening eyes. "He came home a few days ago, sat us down and said he was taking back leadership of the family."

After a short pause to regain his composure, he continued, "Thank you for putting my Dad back in his rightful place."

The blessing on the cottage porch restored spiritual leadership to a father whose son still needed a spiritual dad.

A Healing Blessing

We received the following note from Doug Hudson in the State of Washington:

Lynn, a few months ago I took your book, *The 2 Minute Miracle*, to a gathering of the church in the home of a friend. There were five or six of us present; one was a lady whose kidneys had shut down and totally inactive for about a year. She was on dialysis and medication with no hope of recovery.

During our time of soaking prayer, I felt it would be good to ask everyone to bless her. We waited on Father, then wrote our blessings on 3x5 cards and took turns speaking blessings for and over her. She was in tears as we did this. We gave her the cards and asked her to read them every day in the morning for herself.

It's been several weeks now. Her kidneys are functioning and she is off medication and dialysis.

Ah! The miracle of blessing!

3

Power of Words

A PONY STOOD ON A SIDEWALK in the middle of Metter, Georgia. My six-year-old eyes had never seen such a beautiful, shiny, black and white creature.

It took some doing, but I finally persuaded my mother to let me ride.

No one was watching when I swung my leg over the saddle, grabbed the reins with the left hand and held my straw hat with the right. I pounded the sides of that creature with my bare heels and shouted, "*Gitty up!*"

The race was on!

Get the picture: A red-headed, freckle-faced farm boy galloping on the sidewalk of a city—shirt tail flapping and shouting at the top of his voice, "Whoopee, gitty up pony!"

When the joy ride ended and the curious crowd of onlookers began to disperse, I slowly got off that steed—exactly where I got on the mechanical pony five minutes earlier.

Plenty of movement going nowhere.

There are two kinds of words: empty words[1] that say nothing and go nowhere, and words that convey positive or negative images.

Blessings are power-words that release energy into people, things and surroundings. I've seen people repent, break free from evil torment, begin their walk with God, and experience emotional as well as physical healing—either instantly or gradually. In several cases marriages have been healed as one spouse spoke blessings upon the other, expressing dormant thoughts and feelings. Such was the case when we met Charles Bevel and his wife, Ramona, during a weekend workshop. Charles seemed very cordial and friendly. Ramona, however, sat down in a back corner of the room with arms crossed, staring at the wall.

In our first session everyone tried to ignore her. Everyone, that is, except Charles, who struggled to conceal his embarrassment.

Near the end of the evening, I demonstrated the power of blessing by taking my wife's hands, looking in her eyes and telling her what fun it is living with her. I assured her of my love and commitment for the rest of our lives.

She returned the blessing in such a moving way several handkerchiefs showed up.

"Does someone else have a blessing to give?" I asked.

Charles was up on his feet heading to the back corner before I barely finished the question. He pulled a chair up in front of Ramona, put his hand under her chin and slowly raised her head until their eyes met.

"Ramona," he said, "I've been a fool to withhold my blessings from you and our three children. I know that I haven't been there for you like I should. Working long hours is no excuse for my neglect. Please forgive me.

"Honey, I bless you for being such a wonderful wife and mother. And cook? You make better biscuits than my mother!

"I recommit my life and love to you tonight. I promise to make time for you and the children and be by your side for as long as I live."

By this time, tears were running down Ramona's cheeks. After a long pause she said, "Charles, I had no idea that you felt that way. Why didn't you *tell* me that you love and appreciate me? All these years I've been longing to be the kind of wife you need."

During our last workshop session members of the group bought a wedding cake, along with a bridal bouquet for Ramona as they renewed their marriage vows before everyone.

Blessing not only conveys God's love but imparts His favor as well. As Aaron spoke the divine name over the people, God said He would be present *in* the blessing to impart blessings to them.[2] This blessing contains *protection* ("The Lord bless you and keep you"), *special favor* ("The Lord make His face to shine on you"), *power and peace* ("The Lord lift up His countenance on you and give you peace"). As amazing as it sounds this spoken blessing actually puts *God's name* on people ("So they will put my name on the Israelites, and I will bless them"), releasing the Spirit of God in their lives![3]

Blessings impart life to children who receive them. Parents who bless their children on a regular basis can expect very positive results. This will build God's character and activate God's covenant promises in their lives.

However, as powerful as blessing is there is no guarantee that God's presence will be received. Judas rejected the blessings of Jesus. Absalom rejected his father's blessings as well. But, blessings aren't easily brushed off because of our natural, inner hunger and need to be blessed.

After a blessing workshop, a father told his family things he learned as they ate Friday night supper. All went well until his teenage son, Tim, complained that he was bored and wanted to leave the table and watch television.

"You can go in a minute, but I want to bless you first." Tim's father put his hands on his son's head, looked him in the eyes and told him how proud he was to have him for a son. He also blessed him with the words of Isaiah. He said,

"Son, may you be as Ephraim and Manasseh who were doubly blessed. May the Spirit of the Lord rest on you—the Spirit of wisdom and of understanding, the Spirit of counsel and of power, the Spirit of knowledge and of the fear of the Lord."[4]

Tim successfully masked any positive response to the whole evening, including this blessing.

On Friday morning of the following week during breakfast, Tim asked his dad, "Dad, I like that blessing stuff. Are we going to do it again tonight?"

While this teenage reaction might be atypical, it points to our deep hunger for blessings. It's in our emotional blueprint or DNA.

THE WAGON

The Bible records and demonstrates how words carry or convey messages—either positive or negative. Proverbs encourages us to use words wisely.

- With his mouth the godless destroys his neighbor, but through knowledge the righteous escape.[5]

- Reckless words pierce like a sword, but the tongue of the wise brings healing.[6]

- The tongue that brings healing is the tree of life, but a deceitful tongue crushes the spirit.[7]

- The tongue has the power of life and death, and those who love it will eat its fruit.[8]

The Book of James uses vivid imagery to emphasize the way words affect people and situations, either for good or for evil. He likens the tongue to a horse's bridle or the rudder of a ship.[9]

Words charged with such potential power can initiate either a curse or a blessing.

Lamar felt called to be a minister and attended Mercer University where we became friends.

After graduation, he began speaking in small country churches to develop his preaching skills.

One Sunday morning, an old man came through the front door where Lamar was shaking hands with members of the departing congregation. He looked at the young preacher and said with disgust in his voice, "You call yourself a preacher. Hah!"

"This comment and subsequent conversation was so traumatic that Lamar never preached again!" his father told me 23 years later.

Jesus demonstrated the power of words years ago as storms, fig trees, demons and dead people responded to his voice.

To encourage us to exercise faith and use divine authority available through Him, Jesus challenged us with the art of mountain moving by speaking in faith to unmovable things.[10]

Was He speaking figuratively or making a literal reference to the power of faith released by words? Recall the time when His words to a fig tree brought instant results[11] or later, when Peter said to a lame beggar, "In the name of Jesus Christ of Nazareth, walk." Instantly the man's ankles and feet became strong as he jumped to his feet and began to walk.[12]

Blessings are beneficial as they are received and understood through words. Words are like wagons because they carry creative power, seeds, thoughts, feelings and messages.

Words Carry Creative Power
God created the universe by speaking it into

existence. Seven times He said, "Let there be" and there was! *This ability to speak things into existence is how we are like God.*

Jesus affirmed this divine nature in man by quoting Psalms 82 when God said, 'You are "gods"; you are all sons of the Most High.'[13]

Far from being magical, words create good or bad, life or death.

Bill Glass tells of the occasion when a mother introduced her children to him.

"This is my little girl. She's very timid."
And the little girl stood with her finger
in her mouth.
"This is my little boy. He's a bully." Sure
enough, there he stood with chest out,
muscles flexed, frowning like a bulldog.
"This is my other little boy. He's very
dumb."
There he stood with a dumb look on his
face.[14]

Those children were becoming creations of their mother's words. Since life and death are in the power of the tongue, we are told to speak life that creates good character, self-worth and noble destiny in our children and grandchildren, as well as people around us.

We'll see in a moment that we are called to even bless troublesome, irregular people in our lives.

Words Carry Seeds

Seeds produce after their kind; you can't get pine trees from grass seed. Words produce in like manner often with a noticeable impact on a person—immediately visible at times, slowly sprouting at other times.

Ron discovered this after attending a workshop on blessing. With a heightened awareness of the power of words, the next day he shouted to a grumpy mail carrier pulling away from his mail box, "God bless you today!"

Suddenly, the truck came to an abrupt halt and backed up. "What did you say to me?" the carrier asked leaning out of the door.

"I said, 'God bless you today.'"

The mail carrier's disposition visibly changed as she smiled and said, "Thank you. That's the nicest thing I've heard all day."

On a larger scale, one can see the effects of these word-seeds in the negotiations for the release of Hebrew slaves in Egypt. While the biblical record doesn't record all that was said between Moses and Pharaoh, the last thing the Egyptian king said to Moses was, "Go! And also bless me."[15]

Words Carry Thoughts and Feelings

Spoken words reveal feelings, opinions and facts, even clothed in the laughter of joking. Strip away the laughter and you'll hear what is *actually* being said. Matthew wrote: "Out of the overflow of the heart the mouth speaks."[16]

Words also reveal feelings of admiration and affirmation. In a recent marriage enrichment group Harry took his wife's hand, looked her in the eyes and said, "Harriet, you are the most important person in my life. Thank you for being such a good mother and wife. If I had searched the whole world, I would not have found a woman that thrills me like you do."

Harriet replied, "That's the first time in years you've looked into my eyes and told me how you felt. Thank you."

Words Carry Messages

A friend of mine told the story of one of her childhood playmates named Bobby. Over the years he became rebellious as anger, bitterness and resentment took root in his life—against God, his parents and his church. His life became consumed with drugs as he gradually became shackled with addictions.

One day Bobby disappeared.

His brokenhearted parents didn't know if he killed himself with an overdose or was murdered by a drug gang. For two years they didn't hear anything from their son, not one phone call, card or letter.

He simply vanished.

One day Bobby's dad felt the crushing grip of months of pent-up frustration and pain while driving on the outskirts of the city where he lived. He pulled his car off on the side of the road, got out and walked off some distance from the highway. He pointed his finger towards the north and yelled with all his might, "BOBBY, COME HOME!" Turning to the south he shouted in the wind, "BOBBY, COME HOME!" These same words were flung to the east and west.

Two days later this dad heard a knock at the door. There stood Bobby.

Bobby was home.

It didn't take long before his dad asked, "Son, where have you been; what brought you home?"

"Dad," Bobby said, ". . . I was sitting on the front porch of an old shack on the edge of the Arizona desert, stoned out of my mind. A wind started blowing and suddenly grew stronger. Dad, I could have sworn that I heard your voice in the wind, *BOBBY, COME HOME!* Dad, I got here just as fast as I could."

I told this story in a meeting in New Zealand and ask, "How do you explain what happened over 1,000 miles away from where Bobby's dad was shouting?"

A little lady standing in back of the room, hands waving as if she was flagging down an airplane, said, "It's in the Bible in Psalms 104:4."

The rustling pages sounded like a gentle breeze blowing thorough the room. Finally, someone read to the group: "He (God) makes winds his messengers."

Apparently, words carry messages even in the wind.

OPEN THE DOOR

How should someone react to insults or hurtful words hurled their way? In the pagan, hostile society of Peter's day, the common response to hostility was retaliation. But Peter said, "Never pay back one wrong with another, or an angry word with another one; instead, pay back with a blessing. This is what you are called to do, so that you inherit a blessing yourself.[17]

Blessings can take the edge off of hurtful words, stem anger and stop animosity shock waves. Rather than reacting to anger with anger, we can choose to speak words of blessing.

But most of the time we find ourselves in situations where no one is upset or angry. Someone just needs blessing. They need the gift we can give by speaking positive words into their lives.

As we make blessing part of our lifestyle, blessings begin to come back to us. As we bless we are blessed. Spoken blessings change people and the atmosphere around us. They reverse curses, curb anger and resentment, and give expression to friendship and goodwill.

God's storehouse of well-being, happiness, and protection is released in people and us as we speak blessings.

Blessing of Well-Being

Someone with a sense of well-being˘ is not shaken by adverse circumstances. He or she experiences a general sense of wellness, often described in terms of material prosperity.[18]

Blessings of well-being extend far beyond material benefits. This well-being is more internal than external. It's who a person is more than what he has. It's about abiding joy more than momentary pleasure. Well-being comes as someone embraces God's goodness and learns to walk with Him.

A good example of people experiencing God's favor can be seen in India, where 35 percent of one billion people live in poverty. Many new Christians live in the context of open hostility and rejection from family and fellow villagers, yet their living standard rises dramatically once they are converted, even if wages are a meager ten dollars a day. Three things account for this. First, they are delivered from their costly addictions. Second, most experience some kind of divine healing which makes expensive trips to the witch doctor unnecessary. Third, they stop borrowing money (for addictions and for witch doctors) from local loan sharks charging exorbitant rates.

Blessing of Happiness and Favor

Everyone wants to be happy—from Sleeping Beauty to the Hunchback of Notre Dame. But happiness is often skewed by the pursuit of money, popularity, good looks or possessions— none of which guarantee the blessing of happiness. Howard Hughes comes to mind. Although notably one of the richest men on earth, he died a deeply disturbed, lonely recluse.

While happiness is contained in the idea of well-being, it is about attitude or mood more than circumstances. In the New Testament, Paul and Silas were happy even in a filthy dungeon. Their inner state was not entirely dependent upon their external circumstances.

God *is* concerned about our happiness—so much so that He sent His Son to earth years ago to restore our broken relationships, teach us how to be happy and how to walk with God and one another.

This concern for our happiness and well-being was underscored as Linda and I changed planes in Newark on the way to Israel. I checked in with a ticket agent named Nora and asked if our assigned seats could be replaced with ones nearer the front of the aircraft for the nine-hour flight to Tel Aviv.

"Be glad you have seats," she said. "We have overbooked this flight and many people are flying standby."

Satisfied to have assigned seats we walked out into the concourse to await our boarding call some 30 minutes later.

As the crowd began to move toward the boarding gate, I glanced over at Nora. She was making a hand motion that I thought was for someone standing next to us. A moment later I saw Nora looking directly at me, nodding for me to come to her counter.

"Give me your tickets," she said. "Tonight you're riding in my cabin." I didn't have a clue what she was talking about, but handed her our two tickets. After a few moments on her computer, she looked at us and said, "Follow me and don't let me lose you in the crowd. I have to get you past the gate."

Nora began weaving through waiting passengers, ducking under ropes, passing agents at the boarding gate and finally down to the door of the aircraft with us in tow. "Stand here until I get you two seats together," she said.

To my amazement we were standing just inside of the First Class cabin. Surely someone has made a mistake. She must think we are someone else. What in the world is this all about?

After she played musical chairs with three other passengers, she came back to us. "I have two seats in the middle. I hope that is okay with you," she said.

It isn't easy describing an overwhelming feeling.

I sat quietly for a while, stunned by our surroundings. I'd walked through First Class on several occasions while boarding flights, but never sat in one of those wide seats. I was awestruck!

Soon, the Lord's presence seemed to fill the cabin—at least where we sat. A conversation inside me went something like this:

You didn't do one thing to deserve this. I did this to show you my love.

I know, Father.

What aircraft did I put you on?

It's a 777. (Seven is the biblical number for completion.)

Yes, I have completed a major work in your life. And what row have I put you on?

I looked up under the overhead bins. *Row eight.* (It's the number for new beginnings.)

Yes, I'm beginning a new work in you.

Love and favor flew with us to Tel Aviv that night.

Blessing of Protection

Divine protection, or lack of it, is viewed according to a person's perspective of life, God and the Bible. Many non-believers, as well as some Christians, discount any divine intervention in their daily lives. They say either there is no God at all, or He does not intervene in human affairs like He did during biblical times.

However, I believe the Bible is not only true but is a reliable guide for anyone who chooses to walk with God. Events recounted in the biblical record continue to occur today, especially in regard to God's divine protection.

Ray from the Bhil Tribe in India is a case in point. Before the Gospel came to his remote region, Ray sacrificed goats to stone gods and made his living as a roadside robber. Christ arrested him and empowered him as a zealous church planter and overseer of 25 house churches.

On the last day of our Indore, India, meeting, Ray came through the line to say goodbye. As I embraced him for the last time, the word of the Lord came to me.

Speak a blessing of protection over him.

I did.

Two weeks later Ray and two friends were preaching the Gospel in a remote village. Tribesmen with bows and arrows ambushed them. All three men sustained wounds, one seriously. Ray suffered only a slight flesh wound under his right arm.

Even after the attack Ray and his friends repeatedly returned to the village, not only preaching, but publicly forgiving and blessing their attackers. Consequently, many villagers became followers of the Prince of Peace.

One of God's methods of protection is expressed through angels—mentioned nearly 300 times in the Bible. Not only do these holy deputies carry out God's will on earth, but they often protect people from danger and death.

Joel News International reported that on January 20, 1999, several Christian young people in Indonesia were hacked to death by Muslim radicals. When one youth escaped into the jungle, a young girl dressed in white met him. She took him to safety in the village of Hatiwe Besar and disappeared.

Simply vanished!

A good biblical example is the time an angel freed Peter from a prison where he was awaiting death.

So Peter was kept in prison, but the church was earnestly praying to God for him.

The night before Herod was to bring him to trial, Peter was sleeping between two soldiers, bound with two chains, and sentries stood guard at the entrance. Suddenly an angel of the Lord appeared and a light shone in the cell. He struck Peter on the side and woke him up. "Quick, get up!" he said, and the chains fell off Peter's wrists.

Then the angel said to him, "Put on your clothes and sandals." And Peter did so. "Wrap your cloak around you and follow me," the angel told him. Peter followed him out of the prison, but he had no idea that what the angel was doing was really happening; he thought he was seeing a vision. They passed the first and second guards and came to the iron gate leading to the city. It opened for them by itself, and they went through it. When they had walked the length of one street, suddenly the angel left him.[19]

Any discussion about God's protection quickly raises the question, "But how do you explain times when a person wasn't protected?"

I can't.

Hebrews 11 addressed this issue in what someone has called, "God's Hall of Fame"— saints who suffered, were imprisoned, tortured and killed. Why? Because God has a mysterious plan to allow some people to suffer and die *by faith.*

Billy Graham says in, *Angels: God's Secret Agents*: "The latter part of Hebrews 11 indicates that those who received no visible help in answer to prayer will have a far greater heavenly reward because they endured by faith alone."[20]

WADE IN THE WATER

When the two-man commando unit of Moses

and Aaron liberated the Egyptian labor camps, they took an evacuation route through a desert. Amid anarchic uproar God instructed Moses to speak to a rock so sufficient water would flow to quench thirsty people and livestock.

Simple. Just *speak* to the rock.

Moses hesitated to speak in faith to the fountainhead (not believing what God told him). Instead, he struck the rock twice with his staff, dishonoring God and His words before the people. Consequently, Moses' inheritance of a land promised was lost through his silence by not speaking when told to do so.

You may find yourself in dry places of need or want. "Speak to that rock before their eyes and it will pour out its water."[21]

I'm suggesting a fountain of blessing is released as we speak faith-filled words and possess what we already have.

The Ripple Effect

Pambi Neube, a mechanical engineer from Zimbabwe, lived in New Zealand while his oldest son was in England. Both stayed in touch although they hadn't seen each other for six years.

Strangely enough, the son's responses stopped during the last year.

Not a word from his son.

Pambi heard that Linda and I were coming to Wellington to conduct a workshop on blessing. After reading the story of Bobby in *The 2 Minute Miracle*, Pambi decided to shout to his son in England a few days before attending the workshop.

Pambi said, "I shouted to the wind and said, 'SON, COME BACK TO ME; COME BACK TO GOD.'"

While Linda was teaching during the afternoon session, Pambi received a text message from his son—the first contact in over a year.

Hey old man, I might not pick up the phone, but that doesn't mean I don't love you. I can't say everything by text but know that I still respect and admire you.

Is it just coincidental that two days after Pambi shouted blessings to his son that the first response came in over a year?

When we saw Pambi on the next trip to New Zealand, I asked about the relationship with his son since the text message two years earlier.

"Oh," he said, "We're now in frequent contact. Everything is okay."

An Email from North Carolina

God's power was displayed so wonderfully in the account you (Lynn) relate regarding Bobby and his return home after his father had called out to the four winds. Well, I decided to do the same thing this week. In our small group at church, there's a dear lady whose husband got into an affair and left home about eight months ago.

I decided if calling to the four winds brought Bobby home, I would try it for her husband, Michael. I went outside Monday and called out, first binding Satan and all evil spirits and loosing Michael from their hold. Then, I did just as you said and cried, "MICHAEL, COME HOME. COME TO JESUS!"

Michael came back home yesterday!

4

Possess What You Already Have

INHERITING BLESSINGS IS ONE THING, possessing them is quiet another—as I learned years ago as a new pastor in town.

"Hello Dr. Reddick, this is Cliff Walters. Could we meet for coffee?" the voice on the phone asked.

After a few minutes of get-to-know-you conversation in a local cafe, he handed me a folded check. "I'm not part of your congregation, but I hear you need books for your personal library," he said.

Picture the shock on my twenty-something-year-old face as I opened it and read the amount—out loud, "10,000!" (To put this in perspective, that would be about $50,000 today).

"Since this is a large gift that will help make

you a better teacher, pastor and person, I made the check out to your church. I'm sure that won't be a problem."

It was.

I told the church finance chairman about the check. He thought that much money given to me for books would stir jealousy and cause misunderstanding in the church. He would not recommend they accept the check.

His words felt like a bomb exploding inside me—leaving me in emotional shambles of confusion, anger and resentment.

I carried that check in my pocket for three weeks, occasionally unfolding it for yet another look at the amount. Questions interrupted my concentration and sleep.

Stir up jealousy? Agitate the congregation? Was he sure? Does he realize how many books that much money will buy?

Finally, I knew what I had to do.

A phone call arranged a second meeting with Mr. Walters. I briefly explained the objections raised and slowly handed him the well-worn check. "Thank you for your trust and generosity," I said. "But I can't accept it and run the risk of upsetting people in the church."

He thought I'd lost my mind.

Yep! And probably a lot more!

That experience taught me the difference between *having* and *possessing*. I had $10,000 that I never possessed.

Peter stressed this difference between *having* a blessing and *possessing* one in our focus Scripture:

> Never pay back one wrong with another,
> or an angry word with another one;
> instead, pay back with a blessing.
> This is what you are called to do,
> so that *you inherit* a blessing yourself.[1]

The Greek word Peter used for "inherit" means *"to obtain by possessing."*[2] His last statement could read: "so that you *obtain by possessing a blessing* yourself."

This chapter is about inheriting blessings—and possessing them *now*—rather than later or in the sweet by-and-by.

BLESSING FOR NOW

In most Western cultures inheritance is received after someone's death. This bittersweet custom has a few negative implications, one of which can be an heir's subtle or subconscious death-wish for a parent or insured spouse.

Death can have a Cinderella effect, instantly transforming an heir from want to wealth, poverty to plenty, or obscurity to prominence. Death can be like an heir hitting the jackpot!

In Middle Eastern biblical culture there were two ways to distribute property and wealth from parents to children, especially sons. This was done by a will after death as in the West or by a gift while the benefactor was living. Both methods are present in the Bible, but the most prominent manner in which an inheritance passed to sons was by a gift *while the father was alive* portrayed in the story of the two sons in Luke 15. "Father, give me my share of the estate," the younger son demanded. So, the father's property was divided between the two boys and the younger set off on his extravaganza.

The prodigal son's gallivanting led to debauchery and, finally, a pigpen. After some time he came to his senses and started home. At least he could be one of his father's slaves, he thought.

What awaited him was not rebuke and servitude but restoration as part of the family— complete with shoes, signet ring and robe. His identity and destiny were graciously restored by a loving father.

The unfolding events of this saga focus on the steadfast love of a father who welcomed back a returning, repentant son. Imagine the son's surprise when his father made him the guest of honor at his homecoming banquet.

The story of the wandering prodigal who returned to a loving, forgiving father is a story that describes what God is like—good, gracious, merciful and loving. He's eager for everyone to have their relationship restored with Him.

Jesus did exactly that for anyone embracing what He did—taking upon Himself our sins through His agony and death. This historic event opened the door for *everyone* to be put back right with Father God and have their walk restored, severed by our ancient ancestors in a Garden.

As we repent (change mind and direction) and return to Father God, the Holy Spirit comes to live in us.[3] This divine impregnation is the supreme gift that forms our identity and destiny. We get His mind,[4] His nature,[5] His character[6] and His power.[7] These gifts become an onboard internal navigation system. We'll know where to walk, which way to turn, and how to get Home.

There's more good news.

While all these blessing-gifts are for now, our Father does reserve a final blessing after we die. We are invited to live in His House forever![8]

GUARD YOUR HEART

The biblical writers used "heart" as a metaphor for wellspring or source of a person's life. It refers to one's inner self—the control center of thinking and ethical living. Proverbs reminds us to guard your heart, for everything you do flows from it."[9]

If you are a pastor or full-time Christian worker, you are especially vulnerable to attacks on the heart or "heart attacks," An article in *The New York Times* highlights this risk:

Members of the clergy now suffer from obesity, hypertension, and depression at rates higher than most Americans. In the last decade, their use of antidepressants has risen, while their life expectancy has fallen. Many would change jobs if they could.[10]

Guarding our heart is necessary because of our fallen nature of self-centered impulses and unmet needs. Sheer determination and a strong will aren't enough according to the Bible. We are shielded only by God's power as we believe He is able to keep us from falling into our lower impulses. Divine power comes where human faith opens the door and asks for help.

As Christ becomes the ruler of our heart or life, we receive His character, mind, nature and power. But we need three keys to unlock the storehouse of our inherited blessings so we can *have or possess* them now.

3 KEYS TO UNLOCK WHAT YOU ALREADY HAVE

God gave the Israelites the region of Canaan

in the Middle East as an inheritance. A scouting party concluded that the country was rich in natural resources but was inhabited by giants. "Do not go there!" was the majority report that was accepted by the Israeli leadership. Because of their fear and lack of faith, God caused Israel to wander aimlessly in the desert region for 40 years.

A full generation later, some two million people were poised on the eastern side of the Jordan River, ready to move into the land promised by God as their inheritance—an inheritance they could possess *now*. To believe this blessing was theirs' wasn't enough. They had to take it. God's part was to give; their part was to believe they could take the land with His power working through them.

This age-old principle of faith (believing a promise) and effort (acting on the promise) is relevant for today.

The Hebrew word bless (*barak*) paints a graphic word picture of a camel kneeling to eat and rest. Only then can a camel be loaded with cargo—goods that will bless other people.

As we rest in God's promises (some 8,000 promises are in the Bible), we are loaded with blessings as we hear Him speak specific words.

Three keys are needed to unlock the inheritance of blessings you have obtained in Christ but may not possess: forgive *and* bless, ask, and expectant faith. Remember the

$10.000 check that was obtained but not possessed?

*Key #1: Forgive **and** Bless*

The first key that unlocks the divine storehouse and releases blessings is to forgive *and* bless. Jesus said, "But I tell you who hear me: Love your enemies, do good to those who hate you, bless those who curse you, pray for those who mistreat you."[11] Peter underscores this principle to pay back emotional hurt feelings with a spoken blessing.

Forgive *and* bless.

Why isn't forgiving someone enough? Can't you just say, *I forgive him or her* and be done with it?

Probably not.

Forgiving is largely a mental exercise or attitude change. How do you know if you really forgive someone? Are you willing to bless them as well?

Blessing makes forgiving genuine. Remember my struggle forgiving Larry? It wasn't until I was willing to bless him—even at a distance—that forgiving became real. Only as I began to think, speak and bless him, did my attitude change. I forgot about the money.

Blessings will NOT flow without the attitude of "forgive *and* bless" deeply rooted in your life. Jesus makes a direct correlation: if you do not forgive someone who wronged us, God *will not* forgive you![12]

Key #2: Ask
The second key to possessing a God-given inheritance is simply *asking.*
Remember Jabez?

"Oh, that You would bless me indeed, and enlarge my territory, that Your hand would be with me, and that You would keep me from evil, that I may not cause pain!" So God granted him what he requested.[13]

Sound over-simplistic? Unrealistic?
Asking for specific blessings acknowledges God as our source. Far from casually uttered words that might hit the divine jackpot, God delights in blessing those who walk with Him daily—a restored walk made possible by Jesus.
The Amplified Bible captures the meaning of *ask* in the original Greek text. "Keep on asking and it will be given you; keep on seeking and you will find; keep on knocking [reverently] and the door will be opened to you."[14] Jesus concludes by saying Father God gives gifts to those who ask Him.[15]

Key #3: Expectant Faith
The third key to possessing God's storehouse of blessings is *expectancy* or *faith.* His blessings

come on two tracks similar to those of a railroad. One track is God's power; the other is faith (expecting results as you ask). For example, two blind men came to Jesus for healing. "According to your faith will it be done to you," He said. Their sight was immediately restored![16]

There were occasions when lack of faith greatly hindered the power of Jesus. His one ministry failure was in his hometown of Nazareth. His miracle-working power was hobbled when people didn't believe. He was amazed at the lack of faith among people who knew him.[17]

Isaac and Joseph knew about this "faith key" that unlocks the storehouse door of blessings. Isaac added faith to his blessings for Jacob and Esau. So did Joseph when he blessed his twelve sons and two grandsons. These two men are listed in the Book of Hebrews as examples of faith. Their blessings shaped their children's lives.

When you think of faith, past spiritual giants come to mind, saints who either looked weird, talked funny, walked on water or lived in monasteries. These mythic superheroes leaped over tall buildings in a single bound or raised the dead with a single word. Their faith seemed to rush out of nowhere and triumph in every situation.

What kind of faith is needed for blessing? Is it

a mysterious unction of the past or mystical ointment for the present? Does it transform common sinners into elite saints?

Hebrews gives a good definition. Faith is "being sure of what we hope for and do not see."[18] Faith is *seeing* what is still incubating; calling forth what is still in the process; accepting what is still on the potter's wheel; believing as future what is still present.

Faith is drawing a mental picture of the blessing completed. Rather than superstitious voodoo or mind control, this is blessing from deep impressions about the person or situation. Faith is holding firm a mental picture.

A woman repeatedly complained about her husband's lack of spiritual interest. Even after praying for years, she saw no encouraging signs. "Why hasn't Bill changed?" she asked.

I asked her a question in response. "Can you imagine Bill on fire for God, praying with you, and blessing you? Can you see him this way?"

"Of course not!" she said.

"Maybe that's why he isn't," I replied.

As we "see" the blessing fulfilled, your blessing and faith help provide the tracks on which God's power travels. Jesus said to a woman instantly healed, "Your faith has healed you."[19]

Miracles always occur in the field of faith, the supernatural realm beyond reason or logic.

What chance do you have to tap this kind of faith to mix with blessing? Two jobs and several children may not leave time for church. Or, perhaps you've either given up on the religious stuff or never had much interest in spiritual things.

Where does blessing fit into the life of a "non-religious" person? Is this a God-thing for saints only, a goody-two-shoes exercise?

God can use anyone—religious or not—to impart blessings because of the nature of words, our natural abilities and everyone's innate hunger for blessings.

Nowhere is this principle more clearly demonstrated than in the case of Balaam. Although his spiritual state was described as "wicked,"[20] his blessings on the Israelites still had a powerful effect.

1. The Nature of Words

We've seen that words are like seeds and wagons: they produce after their kind and carry messages, thoughts and feelings from one person to another like ripples on water. Furthermore, words can create either good or evil in their wake, setting in motion blessing or cursing.

2. Natural Abilities

Faith is "being sure of what we hope for and do not see." A crucial element of faith is seeing something in the mind and believing it will happen. All of us have this God-given ability because everyone is created in the image or likeness of God. Even an unbeliever, often referred to as "Gentile" in the New Testament, has a God-consciousness and an inner faith to believe things that are not visible.[21]

Anyone can hope for the unseen and hold a picture in mind until it comes to pass. This hope is combined with blessings that flow from one's natural abilities due to the divine imprint or God-consciousness in every person.

Anyone can bless by expressing love, kindness and affirmations that enrich another person's life. A Christian, however, has a decided advantage over the unbeliever who depends on their own abilities. For a Christian, blessings run on tracks of their faith and God's power.

3. Innate Hunger for Blessings

This God consciousness not only gives everyone the ability to bless but accounts for everyone's hunger *for* blessings. Humans are three-part beings: spirit, soul and body. We are spirit, have a soul and live in a body or earth suit. Every part of our triune-nature craves blessings—human and divine.

START NOW!

Knowing you can start obtaining blessings today is one thing; possessing them is another. If you're ready, let's map the course for better physical, emotional and spiritual health. Here's how to begin. Ask the Lord to forgive any negative feelings you harbor. Sitting right where you are, ask Him to bless and show favor on the person who hurt you. Remember it's not enough to forgive; you must begin blessing—in person, at a distance or thinking silent blessings for this irregular person. This clears the way for healing your soul wounds.

Now, ask that your storehouse doors be opened and blessings begin to flow. Expect to see the Holy Spirit move on your behalf. You are moving from unforgiving to forgiving, from hurting to healing, from fearing to believing, from criticizing to blessings, from obtaining to possessing.

Be patient, this may take some time, but change occurring within you opens your hands to possess what is already yours.

THE RIPPLE EFFECT

At the end of a men's workshop on blessing, I asked if anyone in the group wanted to bless someone else. Several men came forward with a friend.

How refreshing to see one man look another in the eyes and speak stirring words! It's not often that you see men in front of other men with tears running down their cheeks.

I didn't hear from George until three years after he left the workshop. Here's what happened.

During breakfast the morning after returning home, George told his wife he wanted to bless her. She thought that was the craziest thing she'd ever heard him say and told him so in no uncertain words.

However, George took his wife's hands across the table, looked her in the eyes and told her how much she meant to him through their many years of marriage.

The response wasn't what you'd expect. As he finished she snatched her hands away and left the kitchen in a huff.

On the second morning George made the same "I want to bless you" announcement, did the same thing with the same results.

This familiar scene persisted for eight days. Farmer or no farmer, George knew that blessing seeds he was planting in his wife's life would eventually bring positive results. It's the nature of spoken blessings George discovered from reading *The 2 Minute Miracle* and seeing what happened in the Blessing Workshop.

Breakfast number nine arrived.

George said, "I have another blessing for you," as he reached across the table for her hands. Something happened that morning so remarkable that three years later, George's eyes moistened as he told me.

"The moment I touched her hands, she said that she'd like to bless me too!"

"Lynn," George said, "My wife and I have been blessing each other every morning for three years. Never has our marriage been as strong, loving or exciting."

5

Oh, Come On. Bless Myself? Seriously?

LEARNING TO BLESS YOURSELF often raises hackles among the holy. The teaching, "woe is me; I am a poor sinner saved by grace," echoes through many hallowed pews of somber saints.

However, wallowing in shame and self-humiliation is counter to the mission and message of Jesus. His command is to love yourself,[1] as a new creature in Christ Jesus.[2] These principles of self-worth and self-respect still mystify many Christians today.

The purpose of this chapter is to challenge the false humility that associates shame and humiliation with holiness.

First, we'll look at where many of us are, or have been in days gone by. How do we see ourselves? Why is it difficult to accept compliments? Why don't we bless people around us?

And, the very idea of blessing myself? Are you serious?

We begin with a true story that appeared in *Cotton Tales*,[3] a book I wrote awhile back. Folks in Portal are still laughing about my fuss with Elroy.

THE MAN WHO WASN'T THERE

If you're from a big city and happen to find yourself someday passing through a small rural town like the one I call home, you might be surprised to find fellow motorists tossing up a finger or two at you as they pass. Depending on how big the city is you're coming from, you might be surprised to find it's not the finger you're accustomed to seeing. That's one of those nice things about being out in rural America; you're surrounded by good, hard-working folk who aren't too busy or preoccupied to nod or wave, even to a passing stranger.

I grew up near Portal, and I know many of the people here. But I went off to college and spent the bulk of my life living in various cities up and down the eastern U.S. (Yes, I've seen my share of big-city fingers, too).

Now that I've moved back where I grew up, I

can appreciate even more the friendly, passing gestures among members of this great community.

However, over the last couple of weeks I've had several encounters with a local man who has refused to return my greetings, all the while looking me dead in the eye. I don't mean to put down city-life or city-folk, but had something like this happened in, say, downtown Atlanta, I wouldn't have thought twice about it. Sometimes being friendly with strangers can open hatches that are better left battened down. Understandably, people are often guarded.

The local man in question tends a fruit and vegetable stand located in a roadside yard just within the city limits. I pass him every time I go into town and again when I return.

At first when I saw him I would simply lift a finger off the steering wheel as I went by, maybe throw in a nod, but he wouldn't acknowledge me, which was okay for a while.

After a few days I began to make speculations about the fellow. Maybe he's got a cataract; maybe he's lost in his own little world. Maybe he's going through some sort of crisis, perhaps a medical condition or a family tragedy.

I decided to conduct a test, see if I could get a better reading on his disposition.

So I became more elaborate with my gestures of greeting. Before long I was lowering my window ahead of time, slowing down, and then throwing my hand out as I passed. I'd shout, "Mornin'!"

But he wouldn't stir.

In a situation like that, about all you can do is shake your head and think, *Wow... unbelievable.*

I think a part of me became, in a sense, intrigued by this guy, this man in a position of public service who seemed to have the personality of a pine tree. He began to enter my thoughts at unexpected times during the day.

Any time I got in the pickup truck to go anywhere, he'd immediately spring to mind because I knew without a doubt that he'd be there, waiting. He always was—daybreak to dusk—without fail.

Finally, I made up my mind and even told Linda that I was going to get to the heart of this matter, regardless.

That morning on my way into town I saw him there, just like always. As I passed I honked the horn real good a couple times and threw my arm out the window.

He didn't budge.

I smiled and thought to myself, *Okay, you just gimme a minute. I'll be right back.*

I took care of some business at the office, made a stop at the post office and then climbed back in the truck. I sat there a moment and formulated my next step.

When I pulled back out onto Highway 80, I remember thinking, *Okay boys, it's show time.*

As I came up on the fruit stand I began steering the truck onto the shoulder of the road, taking it nice and easy. The suspense was killing me, but I kept a cool exterior. I brought the truck to a halt on the edge of the yard, right in front of him.

"Mornin'!" I hollered, grinning ear to ear as if to say, *Bet you won't be ignoring me now.*

Incredibly, he just sat there and didn't say a word.

I kept on grinning and gritting my teeth, holding it in, thinking, *I am not believing this guy.*

A moment or so passed and then the whole thing just began to be too unnerving. He was as unflappable as anyone I'd ever seen. I decided to be direct with him. Just get straight to the point:

"Do you have a problem with me, friend?"

Nothing.

Okay, that does it, I thought.

I stepped out of the truck and began making my way up the grassy incline. Halfway to the stand, I looked up to meet his eye. And stopped—

All I could do was stand there for a moment and shake my head.

"Unbelievable," I said.

I glanced around to see if anyone was looking. The coast was clear so I spun back toward the truck and climbed in and headed home.

Linda saw me coming up the dirt lane and greeted me on the front porch.

"How did it go?"

"Well," I said, "I guess you could say he won. I won't be waving at him anymore."

"Why is that?"

"Because..." I hesitated. Then I just said it: "Because he's a dummy, that's why."

"Lynn Reddick, I am shocked at you! What a terrible thing to say."

But it was true. That man, a product of the modern world, had good reason to have such a vacant look in his eyes, such a blank expression—for he was in fact, a mannequin (I found out later he goes by the name, "Elroy"), a true-to-life dummy.

Yep, felt like I'd fallen out of the tree of good sense and hit every limb on the way down. Stupid me!

Sound familiar?

Our past fears, failures and fumbling are the trio shouting: *See there, you did it again!*

WEEDING OUT NEGATIVE THOUGHTS

Why do we often talk to ourselves in degrading ways? Somewhere in our brain there's a garden spot where thoughts are planted. Some lie dormant for years while others sprout quickly into attitudes and behavior—good or bad. Perhaps this explains the Proverb: *As a man thinks in his heart, so is he.*[4]

For most of us negative thoughts are invasive thieves that steal peace of mind, joy, happiness, contentment, energy and health. To correct our thinking, our inner self must be reconstructed.

Enter Christ the Carpenter.

He doesn't remodel our inner self. He clears out the debris of past sin, shame and guilt and constructs something new. After we become a new person in Christ[5] and receive the Holy Spirit inside,[6] there is still work to be done as we "put on the new self."[7] Paul says our mind and thoughts must be renewed through a process of cleansing and reprograming[8] so negative thinking no longer chokes positive thoughts in our mental garden.

Sound too good to be true? Not if our perspective changes so we begin to see ourselves in a different light.

The person who experiences the new birth and becomes a different person carries the anointing of the Holy Spirit.[9] This power and presence enables a Christian to continue the work of Jesus. Not only is it a new day, it's a new identity and destiny.

This paves the way to begin thinking, feeling, seeing and acting like a man or woman of God. It's difficult to love and bless other people if you don't love and bless yourself.[10]

The practice of blessing ourselves is reinforced in these words: "He who blesses himself in the earth shall bless himself in the God of truth."[11] Isaiah says we are to agree with what God says about us, since He is the "God of truth."

It's not every day that we meet an Elroy on the side of the road that causes us to say to ourselves, "That was about the dumbest thing I've ever done." But, if not Elroy, it's usually someone or something that causes negative thoughts to spring up in our mental garden.

Thinking, speaking and giving blessings are tools to remove mental weeds so God's love can flourish in us—like turning a graveside canopy into a revival tent.

God's love, expressed through someone, not only gives us value but stirs inner gifts and abilities that are dormant or smothered by failure, guilt, or rejection. This self-worth comes from God who commands us to love ourselves and bless ourselves in the God of truth.

Start blessing yourself as the person you are in Christ Jesus.

Seriously!

THE RIPPLE EFFECT

Harry Strikes It Rich

Harry's company was on the verge of financial ruin, hounded by suppliers and bankers demanding money he didn't have.

An old man found Harry sitting on a park bench with head buried in his hands thinking, *what in the world am I going to do?*

"I see something is troubling you," the old man said.

It didn't take long for Harry to describe his financial woes.

"I believe there's something I can do. What is your name?" he asked as he wrote out a check. "Take this money and meet me one year from today—same time and place. You can pay me back then.

When Harry finished staring at the check for $500,000 and looked up, the old man was gone as suddenly as he appeared. The signature on the check was John D. Rockefeller, one of the richest men in the world!

I can erase my money worries in an instant! He realized. But instead, Harry decided to put the uncashed check in his safe. Just knowing it was there might give him strength to figure a way to save his business.

Harry's renewed self-confidence and optimism did wonders. His new lease on life attracted new customers and better business deals. In six months he was out of debt and making money.

Exactly one year later, he returned to the park with the uncashed check just as the old man came hobbling down the sidewalk. It didn't take Harry long to tell his success story and express his thanks for the man's confidence in him.

Just as Harry reached in his pocket to get the check, a nurse came running up and grabbed the old man.

"I'm so glad I caught him!" she said. "I hope he hasn't been bothering you. He's always escaping from the nursing home and telling people he's John D. Rockefeller."

The old man looked back and smiled over his shoulder as she led him away by the arm.

Harry stood there stunned.

He'd been wheeling and dealing all year, convinced $500,000 was backing him up. But, it wasn't the money, real or imagined, that brought new life and success. It was belief in his inner resources and in the confidence instilled in him by another person's blessing.

6

12 Times to Bless

ANYTIME IS A GOOD TIME TO BLESS God, people, things or yourself.

Perhaps you've asked, "How do I bless? What do I say, or how do I begin?"

The following five steps[1] can help start your journey, silence your fears and stir your authority and power to bless.

HOW TO BLESS SOMEONE

You have probably heard the old adage, 'Actions speak louder than words.' While that may be true in most cases, combining actions with words can be a powerful life-changing event.

Blessing molds actions and words into an awesome avenue to speak prophetic identity and destiny into your friends and family.

Here's a simple step by step method we

use to bless people. Remember that Jesus spoke with simple word pictures.

So let's get started.

1. Touch the Person, If Appropriate.

Begin by making contact with the person you want to bless, holding hands or placing your hand on their shoulder. Be aware that some people shrink at being touched, and it may make them uncomfortable at first. It may be a good idea to ask permission before touching them. You can say, "Would it be ok if we hold hands?" or "Can I put my hand on your shoulder?"

2. Look Them In the Eyes

The eyes are the window to the soul. You want your words to have an impact on their future. Not looking at them can send a message of insincerity. However, people in some cultures are not accustomed to eye contact, but blessing can overcome this custom.

3. Speak About Their Identity

Call them by name, tell them what they mean to you, and how they have blessed your life and others. This expresses how you see them and gives them a sense of worth.

4. Tell Something of Their Destiny

This is a major faith leap for some people because they have not been taught how to listen to the Holy Spirit. Here is where the word pictures come into play.

For example, you may get a mental image of this person that resembles a tree. You could say,

I see you as a beautiful maple tree; its branches filled with brightly colored leaves, its sap sweet to the taste, its branches a safe haven for the birds, its shadow giving shade to the weary. I see Father expanding your branches giving you farther reach, making your sweetness into an irresistible draw to the lost. Your majestic height is a beacon that can be seen from afar.

This word picture can be as detailed or brief as you want. Remember, you're the one giving the blessing. It is important to understand that this prophetic element of the blessing is probably the most important part. It speaks to a person's future, helping them change the way they see themselves or, more importantly, how Father God sees them. Words of identity reflect how you see an individual and words of destiny reflect how God sees them. This may not be a picture of their present condition, but what the Holy Spirit wants to pour into their lives.

5. Assure Them of Your Help

You can give the person assurance of your steadfast support and prayers as the Holy Spirit works in them. Some words of destiny can impact the person so deeply that your commitment of support is a great comfort, especially as they begin to wrestle with this new facelift for their life.

A hug is usually a great way to complete the blessing. We've found it helpful to have a box of tissues handy during a blessing because many people may have never heard affirming words before. When they finally encounter affirmation their eyes begin to leak!

When the Allied Troops were slugging it out in the mountains of Sicily during WWII, General Bradley said of General George Patton, "Give George a newspaper headline and he is good for another fifty miles." Mark Twain once said, "I can live two months on a good compliment."

Words of affirmation never go out of style!

SPECIAL EVENTS FOR BLESSING

The question was asked during one of our workshops, "Does anyone have a blessing for someone in the group?"

Tom Farrar quickly turned to his wife, Nelda, and said, "I want to do something I've never done during the 40 years we've been married. You know that I wasn't raised this way, but I'm going to bless you if it kills me."

Tom struggled as love and admiration for Nelda slowly surfaced in his blessing. He continued to affirm her for several minutes.

"From this day on," he assured her, "I'll bless you *every* day for the rest of our lives."

"Tom, that's the best news I've heard in years!" Nelda said.

Tom and Nelda were among the last to leave the room, but not before he said to me, "This has been the most significant day of my life."

"Nelda," I said, looking at Tom, "Every time I see you, I'm going to ask if he's still blessing you."

A few months later the couple registered for a three-day camp we scheduled near Chicago. Across campus I recognized Tom and shouted a hello, but wasn't sure who the woman was with Him. It didn't look like Nelda. I wondered what happened.

Quickly, I walked toward them still puzzled about this unfamiliar woman with him. After greeting Tom, I said, "Is that you, Nelda?"

It was.

I could hardly believe daily blessings had changed her looks that much. One is reminded of Eliza Doolittle's comment in the Broadway musical, *My Fair Lady*. "The difference between a princess and a flower girl is how she's treated."

While Tom discovered that *anytime* is a good time to bless Nelda, there are twelve special times blessing can release God's power, goodness, favor and protection into someone's life.

1. Conception and Pregnancy

An unborn child's ability to receive messages and stimuli outside the womb has been documented by modern research. The Bible notes this in Elizabeth's words to Mary. "As soon as the sound of your greetings reached my ears, the baby in my womb leaped for joy."[2]

Spoken blessings begin to shape the child's identity and destiny even in the womb. They can also be spoken over parents-to-be.

Jeremiah is an example of being blessed before he was born. God said to Jeremiah, "Before I formed you in the womb I knew you, before you were born I set you apart; I appointed you as a prophet to the nation."[3] If God blessed unborn Jeremiah with an anointing, we would do well to follow His example by frequently blessing unborn children.

I had an opportunity to exercise this kind of blessing when our daughter became pregnant. The first few months of pregnancy went as we hoped: full of excitement and positive test results. Then in the sixth month, Laura went into labor. This crisis forced her onto hospital bedrest for the next three months.

In response to a phone call, Linda and I quickly drove to the hospital. Many troubling questions came to mind. Is Laura on the verge of a miscarriage? Is she going to have a premature child? Is this a physical or spiritual battle we're facing? Or both?

Seated around the hospital bed among the gathering of her husband and friends, my mind kept going back to the words Jesus spoke about faith.

> Have faith in God. I tell you the truth, if
> anyone says to this mountain, 'Go throw
> yourself into the sea,' and does not doubt
> in his heart but believes that what he
> says will happen, it will be done for him.[4]

Why couldn't that authority be used with our unborn granddaughter? I wondered.

When a lull came in the conversation something welled up in me. I moved closer to the bed and placed my hand on Laura's stomach and spoke to the child in her womb: "Honey, this is your Papa. Don't come out yet. It's not time." I paused. Stillness had settled in the room. I felt a strong sense of peace settling over me as well. I leaned in closer yet, and spoke the words again; "This is Papa. Don't come out yet. Now is not the time."

I continued this one-sided conversation with our unborn granddaughter until week 37 when Kayla came out of the womb, healthy six pounds, six ounces.

2. Birth/Birthdays

The angel Gabriel said that John the Baptizer would be filled with the Holy Spirit "even from birth."[5] When he was born relatives and neighbors gathered to "magnify" the Lord[6] and rejoice together. Blessings are clearly inferred in magnifying God and rejoicing with parents.

Similarly, Paul's testimony of early blessings included his gratitude that God "set me apart from birth and called me by his grace."[7]

Minutes after our grandson was born, I held him in my arms and said, *"Ethan, I'm so proud you're in our family. I bless you with God's presence. May you be a mighty man of God, full of joy and peace."*

3. Weaning

Weaning can be a threat to a baby's sense of well-being, since milk is the child's earliest association with love. Weaning is more about detachment, either from bottle or breast, than about milk. It's hard to imagine the emotions of insecurity and separation that are likely stirred when the pattern of physical touch and stimulation is abruptly stopped through the weaning process.

Frequently spoken blessings can bring reassurance that the child is not being rejected as the bottle or nipple is taken away. This crucial time in the child's emotional development can threaten intimacy with the mother as well.

Weaning—whether done early or in the fourth or fifth year as in many non-Western cultures—can be accompanied by an Abraham-style party. "The child grew and was weaned, and on the day Isaac was weaned Abraham held a great feast."[8] While not specifically stated in this text, we know from Hebrew traditions that blessings played a large role in such weaning feasts.

After weaning, the child is free to continue the growth and development process, moving into the area of separateness. In fact, this is what weaning is all about—the child begins to see himself or herself detached from mother with a separate identity.

4. Beginning of School

School usually begins at a specific time and age. I still remember the first morning I stood outside my house and watched the big yellow monster approaching, ready to gobble me up.

As it came to a stop, its mouth squeaked open. I looked up and saw a man who seemed to be seated on a throne, peering down at me over his horn-rimmed glasses.

"Get in, boy!" he said.

I could have used a blessing that day to help ease my adjustment to new faces, old fears, and frightful places.

5. *Puberty*

Most adolescents don't see themselves as emerging adults due to rapid and radical physical, social and emotional changes. At what point does a child see himself or herself as an adult?

Almost every culture marks the transition from childhood into adulthood with a "rite of passage." This *rite* is a ceremony, ritual, service or observance that usually comes from cultural traditions performed in a few hours or over several months. A *passage* is a voyage or journey from childhood into early adulthood expressed in some kind of ceremony.

At puberty the father—more than the mother—plays the key role in confirming a child's identity and releasing the son or daughter into their destiny. A father's blessings are so important that Jesus didn't begin his ministry or perform one miracle until his heavenly Father said, "You are my Son, whom I love; with you I am well pleased."[9] Many Jewish fathers speak this blessing over their sons during the bar mitzvah rite of passage today!

Various religious traditions welcome people differently into their faith community, usually around the time of puberty. Whether by confirmation, public confession of faith and baptism or some other initiatory act, blessings should be given by members of that community during this time.

Jesus went to the Jerusalem Feast of Passover with his parents when he was twelve years old. Some scholars have concluded that he turned thirteen while in Jerusalem and was initiated into the community of faith with a bar mitzvah ceremony. That might explain his participation in adult discussions in the Temple.

Details of a bar mitzvah are not recorded in the Bible, but religious traditions surrounding this ancient rite of passage include instruction, ceremony, blessing and celebration.

A Texas couple carefully designed a day-long rite of passage for their thirteen year-old son with family and friends. As the mantle of night fell, the dad asked his son to get a flashlight and join him for a walk.

During the half-mile stroll his father spoke blessings over him. No conversation, just dad blessing his son until they came to a conspicuous ribbon tied on a tree limb. As they stopped to examine it, dad shined the light in a clump of nearby bushes. Out popped the son's baseball coach who was the second important man in his life.

The coach took the flashlight and asked the boy to walk with him. Only blessings were spoken into the boy's life for the next half-mile until they came to a second ribbon waving in the cool night breeze. As they stopped the coach shined the light on the boy's pastor leaning against a tree. He took the light and asked the boy to continue the walk.

This journey of blessing continued until five men had spoken into that boy's life on the night he would *never* forget.

6. *Children Leave Home*

Blessings spoken over children leaving home occurs numerous times in the Bible. In these instances, blessing helped shape the identity and destiny of the departing family member. Departing blessings were spoken by Isaac,[10] Laban,[11] Jacob,[12] Jethro,[13] and Rebekah's family[14]—to name only a few.

When a child leaves home, blessings from family members help ease the adjustment to school, work or living conditions. Blessing gives confidence, encouragement and "you-can-do-it" assurance.

Before Jacob left his father's house, Isaac spoke a farewell blessing over him even though Jacob had deceived him. Isaac's farewell blessing for Jacob was this:

May God Almighty bless you and make
you fruitful and increase your numbers
until you become a community of peoples.
May he give you and your descendants

the blessing given to Abraham, so that
you may take possession of the land
where you now live as an alien, the land
God gave to Abraham.[15]

7. Marriage

We hear blessings during wedding festivities
more frequently than other times. These
expressions of health, happiness and long life
vary from jovial toasts to solemn ceremonies.

The Bible makes little reference to blessings
during weddings. There is one reference to
blessing at a wedding supper when John said
that those who attend the wedding supper of the
Lamb are blessed.[16] However, the Torah forbids
a newly married man to leave for war during the
first year of marriage, so he can "bring
happiness to the wife he has married."[17] In
Hebrew traditions blessing a wife is part of her
happiness.

Israel's elders blessed Boaz just prior to his
marriage to Ruth:

May the LORD make the woman who is
coming into your home like Rachel and
Leah, who together built up the house of
Israel. May you have standing in Ephratah
and be famous in Bethlehem. Through
the offspring the Lord gives you by this
young woman, may your family be like that
of Perez, whom Tamar bore to Judah.[18]

Wedding festivities are excellent times when blessings are needed, both for the couple as well as parents left in the "empty nest."

8. Spiritual Encounters

The Bible records numerous spiritual encounters or holy ambushes when blessings were spoken by God or by angels.

Jacob is a case in point. His brother's rage drove him to a desert resting place where God appeared to him in a dream and blessed him. When Jacob awoke, he in turn, blessed God and the spot he named Bethel, "House of God."[19]

As Jacob was returning home 20 years later, he wrestled with a spiritual being all night. At daybreak the "man" said, "Let me go."

Jacob replied, "I will not let you go unless you bless me."

This requested blessing changed his name from Jacob (One who supplants) to Israel (One who strives with God). Jacob blessed the place of spiritual encounter by calling it Peniel, "Face of God."[20] Jacob spoke blessings over both places he regarded as holy.

In the New Testament the Damascus road experience not only changed Saul into Paul, but one who persecutes into one who blesses.

9. Significant Accomplishments

Before departing on an extended trip, a master gave his money to three servants. To one he gave $5,000 dollars to invest during his absence. When the man returned he learned that the wise investor had doubled his money. This accomplishment resulted in a spoken blessing: "Well done, good and faithful servant! You have been faithful with a few things; I will put you in charge of many things. Come and share your master's happiness!"[21]

Here's part of a public blessing I gave my brother at a military pinning ceremony.

> *Terrell, I bless you as Brigadier General. You command your troops with wisdom, compassion, and genuine concern. They hold you in high esteem. It is not by accident that such a large number was present at your Changing of the Guard Ceremony a few weeks ago.*
>
> *I bless you as my brother. You have always "been there" for me. I have benefited from your wisdom, counsel, and generosity.*
>
> *There is a bond that exists between us that has nothing to do with accomplishments, status, or money. It is a covenant bond that says "What is mine is yours, and what is yours is mine."*

10. Illness

Sickness, whether long or brief, interrupts daily routines for both patient and family. A prolonged sickness can create guilt, grief, and anger in the patient. Frequent blessings spoken by family and friends during sickness can bring reassurance and set a positive environment that aids the healing process.

The Bible gives two accounts of a king in Israel who had a terminal illness. Upon learning of his imminent death, Hezekiah called out to God and wept bitterly. Isaiah then blessed the sick king with these words from God:

> I have heard your prayer and seen your tears; I will add fifteen years to your life. And I will deliver you and this city from the hand of the king of Assyria. I will defend this city.[22]

Hezekiah was completely healed in three days.

11. Retirement

Work was contemptible for the ancient Greek and Roman upper classes, in sharp contrast to the Judeo-Christian understanding of work as a command from God.[23] Paul warmed against idleness in one of his Epistles.[24]

Historically, most people died in their 30s or 40s, excluding the possibility of retirement. However, since current life expectancy in industrial nations has more than doubled, people must plan the years after leaving vocational jobs.

Retirement does bring radical change for most people—from exhilarating freedom to debilitating boredom. This sudden routine adjustment can be minimized as family and friends bless the retiree with assuring and affirming words.

At no time are blessings needed more than during the first year of retirement, especially for people whose identity has been wrapped up in their jobs.

12. Death

Jacob's lifestyle of blessing reached a climax shortly before his death when he blessed his twelve sons the last time. These weren't insignificant rambles of an old man, but once-in-a-lifetime words that told what would happen to them in the days to come. History verifies the accuracy of his prophetic blessings.

Discussing death and dying are taboos in our culture. We're uncomfortable talking about death, especially our own. This denial is portrayed when a man said to his wife, "When one of us dies, I'm moving to Paris."

When someone dies we often hear: "I remember the last thing they said." How significant if *our* last words are those of blessings. Like Jacob whose blessings shaped the identity and destiny of each son, our blessings have a powerful impact on those around us not only when we die, but also each day we live.

An old Rabbi said to his student, "Bless people the day before you die."

"But Rabbi," said a student. I don't know the day I will die."

"Then bless people today!"

THE RIPPLE EFFECT

Dean Cozzens saw the power of blessing while serving as an intern at a children's hospital.

He stopped at the nurse's station to check the present condition of Tommy, an emotionally disturbed five-year-old. The nurse took in a deep breath and said, "Tommy hasn't had a good day and, frankly, doesn't seem headed for a good night."

Dean found the boy sitting sideways on his bed, staring at closed curtains.

Tommy turned a scowl toward Dean before spinning his head back around to the curtains.

He approached the boy, laid hands on his chest and back, and began to speak words of spiritual warfare, not stopping when Tommy let out a groan and vomited.

Afterwards, Dean placed his hand on the boy's head and spoke repeated blessings of affirmation and wholeness, at one point repeating, "Power!" again and again. Even after sleep overtook the child, Dean continued to stand over him, speaking blessings.

Two weeks later, Dean, after wrapping up a visit in another wing of the hospital, decide to drop in on his little friend. As he approached the nurse's station, he saw Tommy playing with a toy truck at the threshold of his room.

The nurse gave Dean a smile. She said, "That's not the same Tommy we wrestled with a few weeks ago. The change has been incredible, miraculous." Now Dean smiled. The nurse added, "And you know, whenever I or another nurse tuck him in at night, he reaches up and puts his little hand on our foreheads, and says the strangest thing."

"What's that?" Dean asked.

"He says, 'Power!' Just like that."

An Email from a College Professor

A copy of the Spanish version of *The 2 Minute Miracle* found its way into the hands of a Hispanic professor at a university in Georgia.

He read what Liza Doolittle said, "The only difference between a flower girl and a princess is the way she is treated."

His two-page email to us detailed how he began to weep for the years he treated his wife like a common flower girl—the throw-away kind seen selling flowers on streets of Third World countries.

His repentance led him to kneel down at his wife's feet. "Forgive me," he said. "I will never treat you like a flower girl again."

7

How To Start
A Miracle

EMOTIONS ARE STIRRED when positive words are spoken. Recent brain discoveries have proven how our emotions strongly influence our behavior and capacity to learn. Stirred emotions supply the energy and drive (motivation) to accomplish plans and goals.

The connection between this ground breaking research and the power of blessing is obvious. Blessing others and the need to be blessed are basic to our emotional being.

2 Minute Exercises

Reading this book changes nothing; you must practice what you learn. For maximum results, make a decision to begin a lifestyle of blessing others that will make them happier and you healthier.

The following exercises will open a world of wholeness—both for you and those you bless.

For You

It isn't easy forgiving someone who has wronged you. But this process is quite necessary if you want to be free from encroaching resentment and destructive bitterness. Before we bless others, we must first ask ourselves if there is anyone whom we haven't fully forgiven.

Try this.

Find a quiet place to sit down. Close your eyes. You may want to focus on the Lord for a few minutes in order to help settle your thoughts and begin moving your mind toward a clear, calm and receptive state.

Ask yourself if there is anyone you need to forgive. If someone enters your thoughts, begin there. Once you decide to forgive, blessing that person moves forgiveness along much more rapidly.

Begin speaking forgiveness before you feel it. Finally, you will feel you have *really* forgiven. Remember my story about forgiving Larry in Chapter One? It usually takes time to emotionally work through forgiveness.

Blessings can be given by thoughts, in person, or from a distance. Either way, blessing gradually changes situations and people because of the biblical principle of forgiving—if you forgive others, God will forgive and cancel His judgment against you.

For Married Couples and Parents

Spend a few moments reflecting on your spouse and/or children. Focus on what they mean to you. Think about your dreams for their future.

It may be helpful to jot down three or four sentences on paper that convey the blessing you have for them, thoughts easily memorized to maximize the effect of your words. Some people use appropriate Bible verses.

Find an opportunity to bless your spouse *even if it frightens her (or him) at first*. Remember, it is most effective if you take their hands, make eye contact and affirm them with blessings.

Blessing your children may be awkward and uncomfortable, but it will have a great impact, especially if repeated often.

For Single Adults

Ask several friends at work to read this book. During a lunch break, let everyone practice blessing each other in a manner similar to the one mentioned above. This will deepen friendships rather remarkably. Don't be surprised if someone says, "I didn't know you felt that way about me."

For Youth

Young people catch the miracle of blessing quickly. Practice blessing one another using some of the same principles above. Not only will this strengthen friendships, it can mend broken relationships.

The first time Charlotte and Angie were exposed to blessing was in a home workshop where they were foster children. These two teenage girls didn't like each other. Each resisted the other and made the family environment tense and difficult for other family members.

During the afternoon blessing session, several people shared blessings of warmth, love and affection. When Angie left the room blessings continued as the Holy Spirit intensified His presence among us.

Soon Charlotte slipped out of the room and returned with Angie. She asked Angie to sit in a chair in the middle of the room. Charlotte sat down on the floor at Angie's feet.

"I want to ask your forgiveness for being hard to live with," Charlotte said. "I have really made it difficult for you in this home. I want to love you, but I don't know how to get along with you. I want to. Please forgive me. I see you as a beautiful person who belongs here. You have such a wonderful future. Let's give our friendship another try."

During her emotional blessing, Charlotte's tears fell on Angie's bare feet. Picture the impact the moment Charlotte took her long blonde hair and wiped Angie's feet!

Angie arose from her chair, embraced Charlotte, confessed her own sins and returned a blessing.

DO WHAT GOD DOES

If you've chosen to walk with God, He has *already* given you the Holy Spirit to be like Him, His mind to think like Him and His divine nature to act like Him.

However, receiving these gifts isn't enough. You must practice doing what God does. The New Testament is the record book of Christ's activities—how He thinks and acts. It sets the standard for all human thinking, speaking and living.

It is God's nature to bless you. Therefore, as you practice blessing, His nature is developed in you. Peter reminds us that "this is what you are called to do."

As you bless, you begin inheriting blessings. The Book of Proverbs states that "the blessing of the Lord makes one rich."[1]

Bless and be blessed!

Your blessings flow from God's storehouse as you make blessing part of your daily life. You do what God is doing in partnership with Him. Jesus said we can do nothing without Him. But with Him, our blessings will have a powerful and often miraculous impact upon people.

Your new lifestyle of speaking blessings will change the atmosphere around you—in your home and at work, even in difficult circumstances. As you bless, God releases His power, goodness, favor and protection—often with immediate results. However, blessing seeds may take time to sprout to become visible.

There is a rich storehouse of blessings awaiting you—blessings you already have but may not possess the benefits now.

Begin today to possess your inheritance. Watch the ripple effect of blessing on you as you speak, on people as they hear, and on things around you—often in a matter of minutes.

Sing A Blessing

JIM RUTZ WROTE A SONG that sums up thoughts in this book. It is sung to the tune of "Memory" from the Broadway musical, *Cats*.[1]

Blessings! May I give you my blessings?
They will heal your heart's sorrow.
They will fill you with fire.
Come touch me,
You'll find my hands are flowing with love.
May I join your hands with God's?

Turning! I can see your soul turning!
You're about to touch Jesus.
He will grant your desire.
He'll strengthen the weakest, darkest part of your heart.
Keep on turning! He is here.

Every age finds millions trudging slowly up to Heaven.
Painful steps on rocky, crooked pathways
And chains that bind and cut them.

Listen! It's a new sound of freedom!

Say goodbye to the old days.
You have suffered too long.
Pack lightly.
Your journey may be rapid and wild.
Let the future now begin.

No more losing daily battles, no more fruitless
years.
No more stumbling down a fearful footpath in
slavery to tradition.

Touch me! Don't be fearful of blessings!
Be courageous and reach out.
Put your hands into God's.
May Jesus be more to you than all the world's
gold.
May I bless you with these hands?

Table of Blessing

A FOCUSED TIME OF BLESSING[1] is best done with the family around an evening meal. Spoken blessings can help "turn the hearts of the fathers to their children, and the hearts of the children to their fathers."[2]

Jewish history shows how the home has always been the center of learning and spiritual growth for children with parents as teachers.

The Sabbath meal serves as an anchor stabilizing Jewish people and insuring that the blessings of Abraham, Isaac and Jacob continue for succeeding generations with the Torah taught, Psalms sung and blessings given. No wonder Christians are beginning to discover these biblical principles surrounding what I call the Table of Blessing.

The Table of Blessing in the home is comprised of four parts: (1) the meal, (2) four visual aids, (3) prayer of Jerusalem's peace, and (4) spoken blessings.

Part One: The Meal

The evening meal is usually the best time for families to pass along blessings, but lunch works well. Regardless of the time chosen, special preparation is given for this unhurried meal. For example, depending on the age and preference of children, favorite dishes can be served that make this meal memorable.

Part Two: Four Visual Aids

After the meal, food and dishes are pushed to the center of the table to minimize distractions. Four visual aids used are salt, bread, wine and olive oil. These involve the family in learning spiritual truths as well as lessons about physics, geography, agriculture, chemistry, and a host of other disciplines.

The father or mother takes the lead in presenting these elements and leading the discussion. This also works in one parent families.

1. Salt

Discuss the natural uses of salt and make spiritual applications. One parent holds up a small dish of salt and asks, "What comes to mind when you see salt?" A brief discussion follows, depending on the age and learning skills of the children. Included can be the sources and chemical composition of salt and how it enhances the flavor of food.

Next, a spiritual truth is drawn about salt and flavor. For example: "Just as salt adds flavor to food, Jesus said that *we* are the salt of the earth. How can we add flavor to the lives of people around us? What specific way can you flavor the life of someone in school next week?" This prompts more discussion and stimulates the thinking of those around the table. They begin to make the connection between salt and the issues they face daily. Some families record each response so different aspects of salt are discussed during the following weeks.

2. Bread

The parent takes the bread, holds it up, breaks it and says, "What does bread mean to you?"

The response: "Bread is used for food" leads the family into a discussion about how wheat or corn is grown, processed and baked.   Children can help grind wheat and make bread for next week's meal and/or learn agricultural lessons by planting corn in a container to watch it grow. The internal elements of each seed can be dissected and discussed now or at a later time.

A spiritual application follows such as: "Jesus said that He is the Bread of Life. We eat bread.

Do you see a connection?" More discussion follows.

3. Wine

The third visual aid on the table is wine (or grape juice). The presiding parent holds up a glass of wine and says, "What do you think when you see wine?" Count on lively responses.

One frequent comment is how wine makes someone feel good. Alcohol abuse can be addressed as well as the natural process of making wine, from planting the vines to the fermentation process. More than one family has put grapes in a tub for children to squeeze with their bare feet as in biblical days.

The spiritual connection between wine and the blood of Jesus is easily made. "Just as wine can make you feel good, what does the blood of Jesus mean to you? How do you feel when you think of Him hanging on a wooden cross?"

At this point, the family could share Holy Communion at the table unless there are religious objections. Many families who incorporate this at the table—as in biblical days—find new depth and meaning in the context of a real meal.

In religious circles where Holy Communion is served only by a designated church official, a family could invite this person to the Table of Blessing for the observance. (In any case, there is nothing in the Bible that requires an official.

That is simply a custom that sprang up after A.D. 100).

4. Olive Oil

"What are some of the uses of olive oil?" asks the leader as a bottle of oil is held up. This question launches the family into the natural uses before spiritual applications are made.

Someone may say, "Oil gives us light."

Now is the opportunity to teach historical truths about lamps used during biblical days. From a photo in a Bible dictionary, each child could make such a lamp out of clay and write their name and date on the bottom. Whether sun baked or fired in a kiln, the lamp could be used on the table the following week. Imagine no electric lights next Friday night during the Table of Blessing. This lab experience will be long remembered and the lamp with their name written on the bottom will be treasured much like the blessing notes Mark Eklund and his classmates kept as adults.

"Jesus said, 'I am the light of the world.' How does Jesus light your life?" This is only one example of numerous questions that compare human light and divine light.

Many families use the olive oil to anoint anyone at the table with a physical ailment. The family joins in the prayer of healing.

The Table of Blessing is also designed to be a place of evangelism. Picture a non-Christian present who receives Christ's touch for physical or emotional healing!

PART THREE: PRAYER FOR JERUSALEM

Jerusalem and the Jewish people are dear to God's heart. Children should be taught their importance and learn to pray that God will bring peace to Jerusalem and deal kindly with His people.

Around the table is a good time for the reading of Psalm 122 that admonishes us to "pray for the peace of Jerusalem." A different version of the Bible could be used with discussion of key words and concepts in that Psalm.

Following the reading and brief discussion, someone prays for the peace of Jerusalem. Parents pray with their children and children learn to pray with their family.

PART FOUR: SPOKEN BLESSINGS

Spoken blessings address two basic questions everyone faces: Who am I? What am I worth? (our identity). Why am I here? Where am I going? (our destiny).

People speak to these two life-issues quite naturally, even when blessing for the first time. There seems to be a built-in sense of how to bless.

1. Husband Blesses His Wife

This is the highlight of the entire Table of Blessing for most people, young and old alike.

First, the father takes his wife's hands, looks her in the eyes and blesses her; not prays for her. He can quote part of the Bible (such as Proverbs 31) and combine it with blessings from his heart, or just speak things that will affirm and honor her, usually about her identity and destiny.

How delighted children are to hear the father express love and admiration to their mother! Such weekly blessing provides security and peace to children.

Many fathers kiss their wives at the end of his blessing to show that love can be expressed before others. One way to ease the awkwardness of this is for the husband to say to the children, "Will someone say, 'You may kiss the bride?'"

One of the most powerful effects of blessing is in containing anger and negative feelings. Can a husband or wife verbally abuse or dishonor one another during the week and bless the other before the children on Friday night?

I doubt it!

Not only will blessing stem anger in the family, it is an excellent guard against marital infidelity. Guilt would greatly hinder the weekly blessing should the husband or wife be emotionally or sexually involved with another person. God has so designed blessing that it will surface hidden things and guard against negative behavior or sin.

Blessing is habit-forming. Soon, the husband will bless his wife at other times during the week because of her positive response to his words of honor and affirmation.

An excellent biblical blessing to paraphrase is Proverbs 31:10-31, using the modern translation called, *The Message*. The wife's name is added in the text to personalize the blessing.

2. Wife Blesses Her Husband

A wife's blessing can be spontaneous or incorporate Bible verses. For example, Jeanie Graves took her husband's hands, looked him in the eyes and quoted her version of Psalm 1:1-3. She said:

Tom, how well God must love you—
you don't hang out at the nearby bar,
you don't mess with dead-beats,
you don't use vulgar language.

Instead, you thrill in God's Word,
you chew on Scripture day and night

You're a tree planted in God's Garden,
bearing fresh fruit all the time,
never groping around,
but prospering in the ways of God.

A wife could add personal words to this scriptural blessing that will affirm her husband in front of the children. This acts as a check against her criticism of him. She, too, will begin to bless him during the week, because blessing is contagious.

3. Parents Bless the Children

Usually the father blesses each child by either holding their hands or placing his hands on the child's head and looking them in the eyes. The blessing is not a prayer to God, but an open-eye declaration of blessing from God through the parent to the child. When he has finished, the mother can bless in a similar manner.

Another way parental blessing can be imparted is for both parents to bless each child together before moving to the next child. Whatever method is used, parents should touch their children, look them in the eyes and speak words of love and admiration.

Some often-used scriptural blessings for children are Genesis 48:20, Numbers 6:24-26, or Isaiah 11:2-3. Personal words affirming a child and expressing how special he or she is to the parents are most effective.

4. Children Learn to Bless

When the Table of Blessing becomes a regular part of family life, children should be given the opportunity to bless their parents and one another.

For some children, this may take a while before they feel comfortable expressing their feelings about their parents, but this will happen in time.

Proverbs 31:28 promises that children will rise up and bless their mother. After both parents have finished blessing, the father could ask, "Is there someone who wants to speak a blessing?" Children will soon take the cue and begin to bless those around the table. These blessings should be positive without any negative words.

Study Guide

Living the Miracle

THIS *STUDY GUIDE* LEADS YOU to study and practice key concepts in *The 2 Minute Miracle of Blessing.*[1] As you begin blessing on a regular basis, it's amazing how blessings start coming to you. This irrefutable law of sowing and reaping is astonishing!

Not only will you experience life-changing attitudes and habits, but the ripple effect of blessing will change people, things and the landscape around you.

I guarantee it!

This study is best done in private with Bible and notepad five days a week for six weeks, then shared in group discussions each week. Group accountability will motivate you to do each assignment and enrich your experience.

Each day, read the section in *The 2 Minute Miracle of Blessing* before beginning the exercises. This will refresh your memory of materials for that day.

Oh, wait. At the end of this study, you'll be living a miracle—giving and receiving blessings that have become the warp and woof in your mental fabric.

WEEK ONE

Chapter 1: WHY CAN'T I JUST FORGIVE? (Isn't That Enough?)

DAY ONE: Chuck's Story

In order to "own" the power of words, recall a situation like Chuck's (either personal or someone you know) when a family member was responsible for this kind of emotional damage.

This is personal so jot down notes in such a way that they are significant only to you. Think the situation through. How was it similar to Chuck's circumstances? How was it different? What were the long-term results? What could have been done to avoid the infliction of soul wounds?

DAY TWO: BURIED HURTS AND EMOTIONAL SCARS

1. Another name for emotional injury is "soul wounds." How do these words make you feel? Is anything stirred when you think about this?

2. A soul wound is often handled this way: We tend to _____ a hurt by mental brooding, to _____ the hurt with other people, or _____the hurt through blame, rather than _____ the hurt by forgiving.

3. Rewrite the meaning of the quote below in your own words.

> *An insult leads to injury, which naturally stirs anger (conscious or unconscious), resulting in a refusal to forgive, which breeds resentment or hate, which produces a curse (physical, emotional, and spiritual harm) on the person's life.*

4. What happens to buried hurts planted in the soil of the subconscious?

5. The body _____ what the mind _____.

6. Can you think of a personal experience like that of the author's pea-planting escapade...

something that you thought was buried but came back to haunt you?

This is personal, so jot down notes in such a way that they are significant only to you. Really think the situation through. How was it similar to the author's circumstances? How was it different? Were there any long-term results?

7. What emerges from buried emotional hurts and withheld forgiveness?

8. What is the biblical distinction between hate and resentment? What is the biblical equivalent to hate?

9. What is produced when the seed of resentment is planted? How is it disguised?

10. Resentment becomes a curse in four areas. What are the areas and the symptoms or outcomes?

11. What happens to an individual that allows hate to take root and rule their lives?

12. What happens when we refuse to forgive? I have to ask myself, is there anyone I have refused to forgive? Who is it? Why? What is it doing to me?

DAY THREE: DRIVE-BY BLESSINGS

1. What decision must be made as a result of a soul wound?

2. How will this decision affect your life?

3. What advantage do Christians have in such decisive moments?

4. Have you ever been betrayed by a friend? How did you handle it? If you had dealt with it another way, what could have been the possible outcomes?

DAY FOUR: FORGIVE *AND* BLESS

1. What are Peter's words of advice to those walking through difficulty, disappointment, pain and suffering?

2. What must happen before you or I can bless someone who has wronged us?

3. Is this difficult for you? Why or why not?

4. Be prepared to discuss Solomon's proverb, "If a man pays back evil for good, evil will never leave his house." Is that true? If so, relate possible examples. Jot down your thoughts.

5. What must you and I do in order to be forgiven?

6. How can forgiveness be accomplished if it is not based on a feeling?

7. What happens to the "forgiver" as a result of forgiving and blessing others?

8. Can you think of a personal experience similar to Mike's when someone hurt you and you had no way to reach the person to resolve the issue?

DAY FIVE: NUTS, BOLTS AND WASHERS

1. Reflect on the author's experience. Who is God calling you to forgive and bless?

2. Do not write down the names of individuals or circumstances. Simply record what this means to you at this time? How will you have to change? How will you be changed?

WEEK TWO

Chapter 2: PAPER BLESSINGS & MORE

DAY ONE: Morsla's story and THE SOURCE

1. What would be the most important words of affirmation that you could hear? Who would be saying them? Why?

2. What is the Old Testament word for bless? What does it mean?

3. What is the New Testament word for bless? What does it mean?

4. How does 1 Peter 3:9 expand the New Testament definition?

5. What did God reveal from the beginning of creation?

DAY TWO: RELEASE THE FLOW

1. What is the source of our authority to bless?

2. What happens when we bless?

3. What does blessing release?

CALLED TO BLESS

4. Many of God's blessings are conditional. What is the condition?

5. What does Deuteronomy 11:26-28 state about blessings and cursing?

6. Not all blessings are conditional. What are some other reasons God will bless?

7. What is the relationship between 1 Peter 2:9 and Deuteronomy 10:8, and your power to bless in Christ's name?

8. Who can bless and when?

DAY THREE: OPEN EYE BLESSING

1. What is the greatest gifts one person can give to another? Have you ever received this gift? If so, who gave it to you? If not, from whom would you want to receive this gift the most?

2. Which response do you think was most helpful to Sue in the Chick-fil-A story? How would you respond: prayer blessing, face-to-face blessing or no blessing? Why?

3. Why are face–to–face blessings effective?

4. Like Jacob, have you ever looked into someone's face and thought it was like seeing the face of God? Who was it? What were the

circumstances? Why did you think it was like seeing the face of God?

DAY FOUR: THE AUTHORITY

1. What is the main purpose of blessing someone?

2. What happens through blessing?

3. What can happen when a blessing is received and accepted?

4. Christ has given us the authority to bless in eight scriptures. Which do you find the most helpful? Which is the least helpful? Why?

DAY FIVE: BLESS IN FOUR AREAS

1. Why are we commanded to bless God, things, people and ourselves?

2. Which area is easiest for you? Which area do you struggle with the most? Why?

3. Have you had an experience blessing a "thing" and saw results? What happened?

4. Have you ever thought about blessing yourself? Do you think that blessing yourself is appropriate? If so, write a paragraph blessing yourself.

If you are in weekly group discussions, this is an excellent thing for each group member to share. This gives opportunity for members of the group to affirm each other after a personal blessing is read.

WEEK THREE

Chapter 3: POWER OF WORDS

DAY ONE:

1. How are blessings different from "empty" words?

2. Why didn't Charles bless Ramona during their marriage? What difference would that have made if he had?

STOREHOUSE OF GIFTS

3. What happens to children whose parents bless them on a regular basis?

4. If you were not blessed as you grew up, how different would your life be if you were?

5. Why aren't blessings easily brushed off?

DAY TWO: THE WAGON

1. Summarize the scriptures from Proverbs and James in one statement.

2. Why is the wagon analogy appropriate to describe the nature of words?

Words Carry Creative Power
3. According to the first paragraph in this section, how are we like God? Why is it important?

4. Bill Glass tells about the mother who spoke curses over her children that were molding their identity and destiny. Do you remember someone speaking negative words over you? If so, begin to break this curse by speaking distance blessings upon that person. Say to them what you would want them to say to you.

5. Think of a time when someone spoke words into your life that came to pass. Were they positive or negative words? Did you think they

were important at the time? Are they significant now?

6. Think of a time when you have spoken words into someone's life that came to pass. Were they positive or negative words? Did you think they were important at the time?

DAY THREE:

Words Carry Seeds
1. Explain, in your own words, how words carry seeds.

2. Why do you think it takes some "word seeds" longer to sprout than others?

3. How should sprout time affect the person planting the "word seeds"?

Words Carry Thoughts and Feelings
4. What is teasing?

5. What is the danger of teasing someone (to both the person doing the teasing and the person being teased)?

6. When is it "okay" to tease?

Words Carry Messages

7. "Words are containers, having the power of life and death (Proverbs 18:21). You have this power within you, the authority to speak in line with God's Word."

Rewrite this quote making it an "I" statement.

8. How do you explain how Bobby "heard" his father's voice in the wind, calling him home? Read Psalms 104:4 in the NIV translation.

DAY FOUR: OPEN THE DOOR

1. What was Peter's advice about reacting to insults or hurtful words?

2. Is his advice effective? Why or why not?

3. What gift can you give that costs you little, but can be priceless to the receiver?

4. What are three ways spoken blessings change people, things and the atmosphere around us?

Blessing of Well-Being

5. Explain the blessings of well-being.

6. What does happiness mean to you?

7. What is the connection to well-being?

Blessing of Happiness and Favor
8. What changes our daily moods and attitudes?

9. Can you explain why the Reddicks were upgraded to First Class on the flight to Tel Aviv? Does God really care about our happiness? How about your happiness?

Blessing of Protection
10. What is one way God provides protection? Have you ever been aware of this kind of protection? If so, explain.

11. Why are some people apparently the recipients of divine protection and intervention while others are not?

DAY FIVE: WADE IN THE WATER

1. God told Moses to speak to a rock in the desert and water would gush forth for some two million Hebrews and their livestock. Rather than obey God, Moses struck the rock in anger.
   Create a short story about someone in difficult circumstances. Show the difference between speaking faith rather than exerting human effort alone.

2. How is the Fountainhead of blessings released?

WEEK FOUR

Chapter 4: POSSESS WHAT YOU ALREADY HAVE

DAY ONE: $10,000 and BLESSING FOR NOW

1. The check given to the author was $50,000 at today's value. Did he do the right thing by returning the check? Should he have challenged the finance chairman and asked the church leadership to accept the money? What would you have done? Why?

2. Can you recall a time when you inherited something but could not or would not possess it? Sometimes we inherit negative things as well as positive things. Examine this concept and jot down a few notes for discussion.

3. What blessings have you inherited *and* possessed? How have you lived out that blessing?

4. The story of the prodigal son is multifaceted. Are you the father in the story? The prodigal? The older brother? Determine how each was blessed. As you see yourself in the story, which

blessing is yours. Jot down a few notes for discussion.

DAY TWO: Guard Your Heart

1. What is the biblical metaphor for wellspring or source of life? Does it refer to the physical organ or something else? What?

2. Why should we guard this wellspring of life?

3. How is this done?

4. A Christian receives Christ's character, mind, nature and power. What does that mean? How is that working out for you? Be specific.

DAY THREE: 3 Keys to Unlock What You Already Have:

1. What is the age-old principle of faith and effort?

2. What is the significance of *barak* and *rhema* in the concept of blessing?

3. What is the first key to your storehouse of blessing? Explain. Why can't you just forgive

someone? Do you have to bless the person also? Why? Why not?

4. What happens if forgiving and blessing are not deeply rooted in a person's life?

5. What is the second key to your God given inheritance? Explain.

6. How does asking for specific blessings affect your relationship with God? Are you like Jabez or the woman at the well in John 4?

DAY FOUR:

1. What is the third key to God's storehouse of blessing? Explain.

2. When did a lack of faith hinder the power of Jesus? Give an example when this was true in your life.

3. What is the definition of faith in Hebrews? What does that mean to you? Write this verse in your own words.

4. What does the author mean when he says, "faith is drawing a mental picture of the blessing completed"?

5. When and where do miracles occur? Why?
Give an example when this happened in your
life.

DAY FIVE:

1. How and why can God use anyone, religious
or not, to impart blessings?

2. What is meant by "the nature of words"?

3. What are "natural abilities"?

4. How and why does a Christian have an
advantage in the realm of "natural abilities"?

5. What is meant by "everyone's innate hunger
for blessings"?

6. To know you can receive blessings and receive
them are two different things. Take the first step
by asking the Lord to forgive you of any
unforgiving attitude you harbor.
   Now forgive the person who has hurt you by
saying the words aloud. Ask God to bless them
and show divine favor.

7. What can you expect from God?

8. What can you expect from yourself?

WEEK FIVE

Chapter 5: OH, COME ON. BLESS MYSELF? SERIOUSLY?

DAY ONE:

1. Why is this idea so offensive to many religious people? How does it affect you?

2. Read the account when the author had a fuss with Elroy.

   Recall a time when you said or did something "stupid." How can you begin to weed out negative thoughts, according to Paul? How is that working for you?

3. What are the tools to remove mental weeds of negative thoughts so God's love will flow through you?

4. For Isaiah, God sees us as His children. We should bless ourselves that way: say what God says about us. Read Isaiah 65:16 in KJV or NKJV.

Write another blessing for yourself and post it for daily viewing for 21 days.

DAY TWO:

Chapter 6: 12 TIMES A BLESSING IS NEEDED

1. How different would your life be if you received a blessing each day?

2. Would you respond to other people differently? How would others respond to you?

3. Write a blessing for an expectant mother.

4. What blessings could you speak to the unborn child? Write an example.

DAY THREE:

1. Write a birthday blessing for someone you know: a child, teen, young adult, or senior adult.

2. Write a blessing for a young child as he or she moves into the stage of independence.

3. What would you say to a child beginning school for the first time? Jot down key points you would include.

4. What blessings do teenagers need to hear? Jot down several key points you would use in a blessing.

DAY FOUR:

1. Write a blessing for a young person as he or she leaves home and family.

2. What are some examples or times of spiritual transformations? When do they occur? Why?

3. Write a blessing for someone you know who is sick. Why not email or include it in a card for them?

DAY FIVE:

1. What are the fears of someone retiring? What blessing could you give him or her? If you know someone, send them a blessing.

2. Have you blessed someone who was dying? Think of someone now and write a blessing for

them. You can speak this at a distance or in person.

WEEK SIX

Chapter 7: HOW TO START A MIRACLE

DAY ONE

Do the exercise described under the topic: *For You*. Write a brief response about the experience.

DAY TWO

How has this book changed your perspective of blessing people?

DAY THREE

How will you live differently after reading *The 2 Minute Miracle of Blessing*? Make a list and review it daily for 21 days.

DAY FOUR

What do you consider the most important

insight or significant experience of this study?

DAY FIVE

Your assignment today is to bless someone and write their response in your notes. Read: HOW TO BLESS SOMEONE at the beginning of Chapter 6.

If you are in a weekly discussion group, use this last session for each member to give and receive blessings. Each person can stand before the group to receive a blessing from others in the room.

Notes & Quotes

This section contains further information given in the reference numbers throughout the book. These materials include notable and quotable resources and scriptures.

In The Beginning
(A Personal Statement)

1. This phrase dates back to the Middle Ages when people believed evil spirits tormented people, animals or things. Priests used exorcism on the demons, a method not understood by onlookers who called this practice, "blessing out."

Webb Garrison in his book, *Why You Say It,* says by the 17th century, tongue-lashing resembles a priest blessing out an evil spirit.

2. Proverbs 23:7, *NKJV.*

3. See Rupert Sheldrake, "The Sense of Being Stared At," *Journal of Consciousness Studies,* 12 (2005) 10-31. Also, Lynne McTaggart, *The Intention Experiment* (New York: Free Press, 2007).

4. Numbers 23-24.

5. Matthew 8:5-13.

6. Ephesians 6:23-24.

7. Matthew 8:3.

8. John 4:1-42.

9. Galatians 6:7.

10. Pierre Pradervard, *The Gentle Art of Blessing* (New York: Simon & Schuster, 2009). 41-42.

CHAPTER 1: WHY CAN'T I JUST FORGIVE?
(Isn't That Enough?)

1. 1 John 3:15: Anyone who hates his brother is a murderer, and you know that no murderer has eternal life in him.

2. Matthew 25:41: Then he will say to those on his left, 'Depart from me, you who are cursed, into the eternal fire *prepared for the devil* and his angels,' *Emphasis mine.*

3. Romans 8:26.

4. 1 Peter 3:9, *TJB.*

5. Proverbs 17:13.

6. Ibid., 20:22.

7. Mark 11:25-26: And when you stand praying, if you hold anything against anyone, forgive him, so that your Father in heaven may forgive you your sins.

8. Acts 17:6, *KJV.*

9. 1 Peter 3:9

CHAPTER 2: PAPER BLESSINGS & MORE

1. Hebrews 6:7; 2 Corinthians 9:5.
2. Galatians 3:9; Ephesians 1:3.
3. 1 Peter 3:9, *TAB*.
4. Genesis 1:22, 28.
5. Matthew 10:13, *Emphasis mine.*
6. Deuteronomy 28:2, *Emphasis mine.*
7. Ibid., 11:26-28: See, I am setting before you today a blessing and a curse—the blessing if you obey the commands of the Lord your God that I am giving you today; the curse if you disobey the commands of the Lord your God.
8. Ibid., 10:8.
9. 1 Peter 2:9: But you are a chosen people, a royal priesthood, a holy nation, a people belonging to God, that you may declare the praises of him who called you out of darkness into his wonderful light.
10. Genesis 24:60.
11. 1 Corinthians 14:3. Paul uses the word "prophesies" in the same sense as blessing—speaking to people to strengthen, encourage and comfort.
12. 1 Peter 3:9: Do not repay evil with evil or insult with insult, but with blessing, because to

this you were called so that you may inherit a blessing.

13. Luke 24:50-51: When he had led them out to the vicinity of Bethany, he lifted up his hands and blessed them. While he was blessing them, he left them and was taken up into heaven.

14. 1 Corinthians 2:16: 'For who has known the mind of the Lord that he may instruct him?' But we have the mind of Christ.

15. 2 Peter 1:3-4: His divine power has given us everything we need for life and godliness through our knowledge of him who called us by his own glory and goodness. Through these he has given us his very great and precious promises, so that through them you may participate in the divine nature and escape the corruption in the world caused by evil desires.

16. Acts 1:8: But you will receive power when the Holy Spirit comes on you; and you will be my witnesses in Jerusalem, and in all Judea and Samaria, and to the ends of the earth.

17. John 14:17: The Spirit of truth. The world cannot accept him, because it neither sees him nor knows him. But you know him, for he lives with you and will be in you.

18. Revelation 1:5b-6: To him who loves us and has freed us from our sins by his blood, and has made us to be a kingdom and priests to serve his God and Father—to him be glory and power forever and ever!

19. 2 Corinthians 5:20: We are therefore Christ's ambassadors, as though God were making his appeal through us. We implore you on Christ's behalf: Be reconciled to God.

20. Deuteronomy 8:10: When you have eaten and are full, then you shall bless the Lord your God for the good land which He has given you, *NKJV.*

21. 1 Corinthians 10:16: The cup of blessing which we bless, is it not the communion of the blood of Christ? *NKJV.*

22. 1 Peter 3:9: Never pay back one wrong with another, or an angry word with another one; instead, pay back with a blessing. This is what you are called to do, so that you inherit a blessing yourself, *TJB.*

23. Isaiah 65:16: He who blesses himself in the earth shall bless himself in the God of truth, *NKJV.*

24. 1 Kings 17:1: Now Elijah the Tishbite, from Tishbe in Gilead, said to Ahab, "As the LORD, the God of Israel, lives, whom I serve, there will be neither dew nor rain in the next few years except at my word."

25. Joshua 6:20: When the trumpets sounded, the people shouted, and at the sound of the trumpet, when the people gave a loud shout, the wall collapsed; so every man charged straight in, and they took the city.

26. Matthew 21:18-19: Early in the morning, as he was on his way back to the city, he was

hungry. Seeing a fig tree by the road, he went up to it but found nothing on it except leaves. Then he said to it, "May you never bear fruit again!" Immediately the tree withered.

27. Luke 8:22-24: One day Jesus said to his disciples, "Let us go over to the other side of the lake." So they got into a boat and set out. As they sailed, he fell asleep. A squall came down on the lake, so that the boat was being swamped, and they were in great danger.

The disciples went and woke him, saying, "Master, Master, we're going to drown!"

He got up and rebuked the wind and the raging waters; the storm subsided, and all was calm.

28. Numbers 20:8.

29. Deuteronomy 28:2-4.

30. Malachi 3:11, *NKJV*.

CHAPTER 3: POWER OF WORDS

1. Ephesians 5:6: Let no one deceive you with empty words..."

2. Numbers 6:22-27.

3. Galatians 3:14: He redeemed us in order that the blessing given to Abraham might come to the Gentiles through Christ Jesus, so that by faith we might receive the promise of the Spirit.

4. Based on Isaiah 11:2.

5. Proverbs 11:9.

6. Ibid., 12:18.

7. Ibid., 15:4.

8. Ibid., 18:21.

9. James 3:3-5: When we put bits into the mouths of horses to make them obey us, we can turn the whole animal. Or take ships as an example. Although they are so large and are driven by strong winds, they are steered by a very small rudder wherever the pilot wants to go. Likewise the tongue is a small part of the body, but it makes great boasts.

10. Mark 11:23: I tell you the truth, if anyone says to this mountain, 'Go, throw yourself into the sea,' and does not doubt in his heart but believes that what he says will happen, it will be done for him.

11. Matthew 21:19.

12. Acts 3:6-8.

13. Jesus quoted Psalms 82:6 in John 10:34.

14. Bill Glass, *Expect to Win* (Waco: Word, 1981), 38.

15. Exodus 12:32.

16. Matthew 12:34.

17. 1 Peter 3:9, *TJB*.

18. Hebrews 6:7: Land that drinks in the rain often falling on it and that produces a crop useful to those for whom it is farmed receives the blessing of God.

19. Acts 12:5-10.

20. Billy Graham, *Angles: God's Secret Agents* (New York: Doubleday, 1975), 96.

21. Numbers 20:8.

CHAPTER 4: POSSESS WHAT YOU
ALREADY HAVE

1. 1 Peter 3:9, *TJB, Emphasis mine.*
2. *Thayer's Greek Lexicon.*
3. Romans 8:9.
4. 1 Corinthians 2:16.
5. 2 Peter 1:4.
6. Ibid., 1:3.
7. Acts 1:8.
8. John 14:1-3.
9. Proverbs 4:23.
10. This quote appeared in the August 1, 2010 issue.
11. Luke 6:27-28.
12. Mark 11:25-26.
13. 1 Chronicles 4:10, *NKJV.*
14. Matthew 7:7, *TAB.*
15. Ibid., 7:11.
16. Ibid., 9:29-30.
17. Mark 6:4-6.
18. Hebrews 11:1.
19. Matthew 9:22.
20. 2 Peter 2:15.
21. Romans 2:14-15: When Gentiles who have not [the divine] Law do instinctively what the Law requires...they show that the essential

requirements of the Law are written in their hearts and are operative there; with which their conscience (sense of right and wrong) also bears witness; and their [moral] decisions—their arguments of reason, their condemning or approving thoughts—will accuse or perhaps defend and excuse [them], *TAB*.

Chapter 5: Oh, Come On. Bless Myself? Seriously?

1. Luke 10:27.
2. 2 Corinthians 5:17.
3. M. Lynn Reddick, *Cotton Tales: Life on the Edge of a Cotton Patch* (Portal, GA: Portal Publishing, 2005), 50-56.
4. Proverbs 23:7, *NKJV*.
5. 2 Corinthians 5:17, *NKJV*.
6. John 14:17.
7. Ephesians 4:24.
8. Romans 12:2.
9. 1 John 2:27.
10. Mark 12:31.
11. Isaiah 65:16, *NKJV*.

Chapter 6: 12 Times To Bless

1. Gene and Dolores Weishuhn have been

blessing people on a regular basis since 1998. Through their instructions and example, people learn the power of giving and receiving blessings. These five steps, based on Gary Smalley and John Trent's work, will help anyone learn how to bless people in a matter of minutes.

2. Luke 1:44.

3. Jeremiah 1:5.

4. Mark 11:22-23.

5. Luke 1:15.

6. Ibid., 1:58, *The Nestle Greek Text.*

7. Galatians 1:15.

8. Genesis 21:8.

9. Mark 1:11.

10. Genesis 28:1-5.

11. Ibid., 31:55.

12. Ibid., 48-49.

13. Exodus 4:18.

14. Genesis 24:60.

15. Ibid., 28:3-4.

16. Revelation 19:9.

17. Deuteronomy 24:5.

18. Ruth 4:11-12.

19. Genesis 28:10-22.

20. Ibid., 32:22-32.

21. Matthew 25:21.

22. Isaiah 38:5-6.

23. Exodus 20:9: Six days you shall labor and do all your work.

24. 2 Thessalonians 3:6-15.

CHAPTER 7: HOW TO START A MIRACLE

1. Proverbs 10:22, *TLB*.

SING A BLESSING

1. Linda and I were with Jim the night before we began the nationwide workshops on open church ideas and the blessing. At breakfast the next morning, Jim read these words that came to him through the night.

TABLE OF BLESSING

1. The Table of Blessing is effective in families with small children or grandchildren by incorporating teachings about agriculture, chemistry, biology and Christianity.
Children see the power of blessing demonstrated around the table where they learn to bless members of the family.
2. Malachi 4:6.

STUDY GUIDE

1. This *Study Guide* is based on work done by

Alice F. Hunt, Th.D., for the 2003 Edition of *The 2 Minute Miracle*. Additional notes for this edition are added by the author.

About the Author

Lynn Reddick is an internationally known motivation speaker and church leadership trainer. He and his wife, Linda, travel extensively throughout North America and many foreign countries, conducting workshops on open, interactive meetings, small group dynamics, and life-changing blessings. He is among innovative church leaders who developed cell groups and interactive meeting ideas in the early 1970s.

His academic credentials include a Bachelor of Arts, Master of Divinity, Master of Theology, Doctor of Ministry (D.Min.) and Doctor of Philosophy (Ph.D., magna cum laude). Although his academic preparation is extensive, his main emphasis is on the application of biblical and common-sense principles in everyday life.

Lynn is the author of two books: *The 2 Minute Miracle* and *Cotton Tales*.

Learn more about Lynn and Linda at www.LynnReddick.com.

Printed in Great Britain
by Amazon

63257252R00119